1 MONTH OF
FREE
READING

at
www.ForgottenBooks.com

By purchasing this book you are eligible for one month membership to ForgottenBooks.com, giving you unlimited access to our entire collection of over 1,000,000 titles via our web site and mobile apps.

To claim your free month visit:
www.forgottenbooks.com/free1302390

ISBN 978-0-428-67084-9
PIBN 11302390

This book is a reproduction of an important historical work. Forgotten Books uses state-of-the-art technology to digitally reconstruct the work, preserving the original format whilst repairing imperfections present in the aged copy. In rare cases, an imperfection in the original, such as a blemish or missing page, may be replicated in our edition. We do, however, repair the vast majority of imperfections successfully; any imperfections that remain are intentionally left to preserve the state of such historical works.

THOROUGHFARE PLAN
for the town of

1796 1996

Non Quim Sed Quid

September, 1996

Executive Summary

This plan documents the finding of a thoroughfare study for the Town of Carthage. Below is a listing and brief description of these findings:

Major Thoroughfares

1. Monroe Street (NC 24-27) - widen from a two-lane to a three-lane cross section between McNeill Street (NC 22) to Vass Road (SR 1802).

2. NC 24-27 Bypass - construct a two-lane facility on new location in the southern planning area to alleviate congestion in the downtown area. This would reduce the number of through trips on Monroe, McNeill and McReynolds Streets in downtown Carthage.

3. US15-501/NC 22 - widen from a two-lane to a five-lane cross section between the Carthage Planning Boundary and the proposed NC 24-27 Bypass.

4. Intersection improvements are recommended for the following intersections: NC 22 & US 15-501, and NC 24-27 & US 15-501.

Minor Thoroughfares

5. Also as a long range proposal: Barrett Street, Ray Street, and Saunders Street should be converted into a one-way pair facility in the central business district.

Table of Contents

List of Tables

List of Figures

Appendices

B - Thoroughfare Plan Tabulation

C - Typical Cross Sections

D - Recommended Subdivision Ordinances

E - Planning Area Housing and Employment Data

Chapter 1

Introduction

Overview

Officials of the Town of Carthage, prompted by a desire to adequately plan for the future transportation needs of Carthage, requested the North Carolina Department of Transportation's (NCDOT) assistance in conducting a thoroughfare plan study. The primary concern of the Town Council was the increased congestion in the Central Business District and if there was a need for a bypass as proposed in the Transportation Improvement Program.

The objective of thoroughfare planning is to enable the transportation network to be progressively developed to adequately meet the transportation needs of a community or region as land develops and traffic volumes increase. By not planning now for our future transportation needs, unnecessary costs to the physical, social, and economic environment may very well be incurred. Thoroughfare planning is a tool that can be used by local officials to plan for future transportation needs, while at the same time reducing the costs to our environment.

The primary purpose of this report is to present the findings and recommendations of the thoroughfare plan study conducted for the Town of Carthage. The secondary purpose of this report is to document the basic thoroughfare planning principles and procedures used in developing these recommendations. This report can be divided into five parts. The first part of the report, covered in Chapter 1, covers the highlights of the study. Chapter 2 and 3 provide a detailed description of the Thoroughfare Plan study recommendations and address different methods by which these recommendations can be implemented. The next chapter, Chapter 4, covers study procedures and findings. Chapter 5 and 6 provide a detailed description of population, land use and environmental concerns that were looked at while developing this plan. The final chapter, Chapter 7, covers traffic model development.

Information that will be especially useful to the practitioners is provided in the Appendix. The principles of thoroughfare planning are covered in Appendix A, a detailed tabulation of all routes on the Thoroughfare Plan and a graphical representation of typical cross-sections can be found in Appendix B and C respectively. Information related to subdivision ordinances is covered in Appendix D.

Background

Carthage, located in central North Carolina, is a small urban community located in eastern portion of Moore County. Carthage is located approximately 50 miles southwest of Raleigh, the State Capitol. The Town is mostly residential, with some commercial development along the major thoroughfares that include US 15-501, NC 24-27, and NC 22.

Highlights

Major highlights of the 1996 Carthage Thoroughfare Plan are outlined below. The Thoroughfare Plan map is shown in Figure 2. Projects included in the 1995-2001 Transportation Improvement Program (TIP) are shown in parenthesis.

1. Widen Monroe Street (NC 24-27) to a three-lane cross section from McNeill Street (NC 22) to Vass Road (SR 1802) for improved circulation of internal traffic.

2. Carthage Bypass: NC 24-27, construct on new location a two lane facility on four lane right-of-way. (R-2212)

3. Widen US 15-501 and NC 22 to a multilane facility from Carthage Planning Boundar the US 15-501 and NC 22 intersection. Also widen NC 22 from the US 15-501 and N intersection to the proposed NC 24-27 Bypass.

4. Realign the existing intersection of US 15-501 and NC 22 into a T-intersection with N being the continuous through movement. Finally resign the widened NC 22 to includ US 15-501 from the Planning Boundary to the proposed NC 24-27 Bypass.

5. Realign the intersection of NC 24-27 and US 15-501 into T-intersection to reduce the number of accidents at those locations.

6. Also as a long range proposal: a one-way pair will be needed after the bypass is constructed. At this time the traffic generated in the future year 2025 will again appr the levels of the existing traffic today. This traffic will be mainly internal traffic and existing Saunders, Ray and Barrett Streets should be converted to form the one-way f to circulate this traffic in the central business district.

The North Carolina Department of Transportation and the Town of Carthage are jointly responsible for the proposed thoroughfare improvements. Cooperation between the state and town is of primary concern if the recommendations outlined above are to be successfully implemented. The plan has been mutually adopted by all parties, and it is the responsibility Town to implement the plan following guidelines set forth in Chapter 3. This plan was adop the Town of Carthage on March 18, 1996, and by the North Carolina Department of Transportation on May 3, 1996.

It is important to note that the recommended plan is based on anticipated growth within the as indicated by past trends and future projections. Prior to construction of any of these proje more detailed study will be required to revisit development trends and to determine specific locations and design requirements.

GEOGRAPHIC LOCATION

FOR

CARTHAGE
NORTH CAROLINA

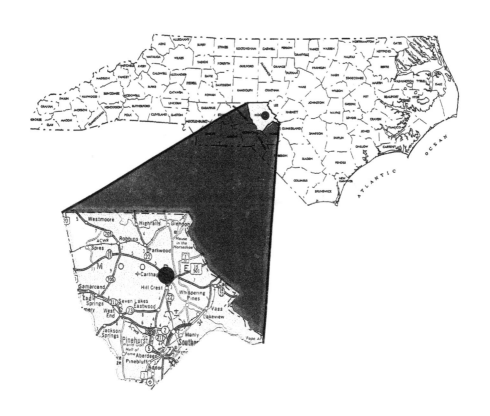

FIGURE

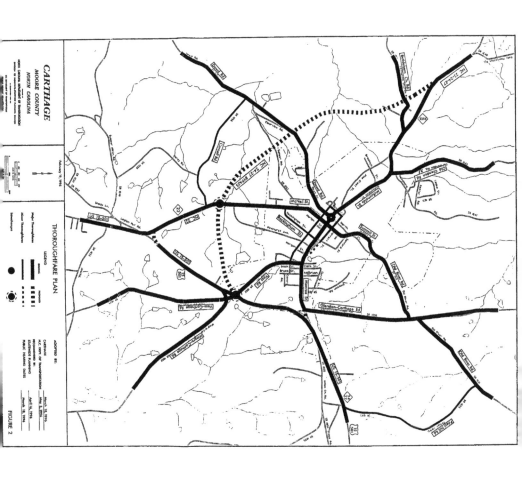

CARTHAGE
MOORE COUNTY
NORTH CAROLINA

NORTH CAROLINA DEPARTMENT OF TRANSPORTATION
DIVISION OF HIGHWAYS

February 16, 1994

THOROUGHFARE PLAN

LEGEND

	EXISTING	PROPOSED
Major Thoroughfare		
Minor Thoroughfare		
Interchanges	●	◉

ADOPTED BY:

CARTHAGE	March 18, 1996
N.C. DEPT. OF TRANSPORTATION	May 2, 1996

RECOMMENDED BY:

STATEWIDE PLANNING	April 16, 1996
PUBLIC HEARING DATES	March 18, 1996

FIGURE 2

Chapter 2

Recommended Thoroughfare Plan

horoughfare Plan

ackbone of a regions economic vitality. Without an adequate transportation
asily reach their intended destination, goods cannot be delivered to the
ve manner, and investors may look to invest in better served areas. Recent
economies, "just in time" delivery, increased automobile ownership, and
ay from the central cities and towns are taxing our existing transportation
nat we put more emphasis on planning for our transportation future.

udy identifies existing and future deficiencies in the transportation system,
: need for new facilities. The thoroughfare plan also provides a
xisting highway system by functional use. This use can be characterized as
ninor thoroughfares plus any new facilities that are needed. A full
rious systems and their subsystems is given in Appendix A.

he thoroughfare plan recommendations. It is the goal of this study that the
forth a transportation system that will serve the anticipated traffic and land
- the Town of Carthage. The primary objective of this plan is to reduce
improve safety by eliminating both existing and projected deficiencies in
rn.

Plan Recommendation

fares

t provide for the expeditious movement of high volumes of traffic within
area.

jor thoroughfare serves travel desires across the southeastern section of the
501 enters the Carthage Planning Area from the east in combination with
ong this section is the Carthage Fair Grounds, the NCDOT Maintenance
ercial developments. Along with the construction of the proposed NC 24-
: section between the eastern planning boundary and the intersection on
be widened to a five lanes in the future year. It is also recommended that
15-501 and NC 24-27 in Carthage be realigned. This recommendation
e grass median and making NC 24-27 connect as a T-intersection at this
cessary traffic signal warrants are met a traffic signal should be placed at

5 15-501 connects NC 22 in the southern portion of the planning area to
rn portion. No improvements have been recommended for this section of
nmended that the intersection of NC 22 and US 15-501 be realigned so that
s into the widened NC 22 as a T-intersection. The new alignment would
at the intersection and reduce the number of accidents at that location.
resigned to include US 15-501 and the existing portion of US 15-501
r or local route.

7

The final section of US 15-501 is from the intersection of NC 22 to the southern planning boundary. It was determined that the volume of traffic on this section of US 15-501 and NC 22 will be over capacity in the design year. It is recommended that is section be widened to a four lane cross section as shown in Appendix C (letter F).

Monroe Street (NC 24-27) - This two lane facility from US 15-501 to the Moore County Court House traffic circle serves as main street for the Town of Carthage. NC 24-27 connects the eastern planning area to the central business district and serves a great deal of through traffic with origins and destinations outside the planning area.

The traffic data in this report indicates that Monroe Street (NC 24-27) is currently nearing capacity from McNeill Street (NC 22) to the traffic circle. Future volumes for Monroe Street in the design year 2025 will be either nearing capacity or over capacity from US 15-501 to the traffic circle. Due to the development and the limited right-of-way along NC 24-27 in this area it is not recommended that this facility be widened to accommodate this future traffic. The recommended alternative is to construct a southern bypass.

It is also recommended that Monroe Street between McNeill Street (NC 22) and Vass Road (SR 1802) be configured to accommodate a three lane cross section (cross section H) to help improve the circulation of internal traffic. The existing pavement width on Monroe Street is already wide enough to accommodate this change and all that will be needed is to resurface and restripe the new configuration to three lanes. This improvement would eliminate back-ups caused by vehicles making left turns in the central business district.

McNeill Street (NC 22) - This radial connects the southern planning area to central business district. This route has a mix of residential and commercial development with most of the commercial development in the central business district. Traffic volumes on NC 22 in the Carthage Planning Area between Monroe Street (NC 24-27) and US 15-501 are beginning to grow due to development in Carthage and in the areas south of the planning area. Because of this development and the proposed construction of the NC 24-27 Bypass it is recommended that the section of NC 22 between US 15-501 and the proposed bypass be widened to a five lane cross section as shown in Appendix C (letter C).

McReynolds Street (NC 22-24-27) - This radial route connects the western planning area to central business district. McReynolds Street has a mix of residential and commercial development along the route. This route also serves a great deal of through traffic with origins and destinations outside the planning area and internal traffic in the central business district. Because the traffic on NC 22 and NC 24-27 combine right before McReynolds Street the traffic volumes on McReynolds Street (NC 22-24-27) in the Carthage Planning Area will be over or near capacity in the future year. Due to the development and the limited right-of-way along NC 24-27 in this area it is not recommended that this facility be widened. The recommended alternative is to construct a southern bypass.

NC 24-27 Bypass - The construction of this facility will reduce the number of passenger vehicles and remove through truck traffic traveling into Town. The construction of this corridor will free up local streets and give local traffic better access to the central business district.

Over the past year, two locations for the Carthage Bypass (NC 24-27 Bypass) facility were looked at to determine the most beneficial facility for the Town and the motorist. The two alternatives that were looked at were a northern bypass and a southern bypass. After doing the analysis, the southern bypass was recommended to the Town as the best alternative for reducing congestion on NC 24-27 in the downtown area. A major reason for selecting this alternative was the southern bypass also would connect to NC 22 thereby allowing an additional 4,000 through trips to use the proposed bypass facility in the future year. The analysis also showed that construction of the northern bypass would be only be a short term remedy and that in the future year NC 24-27 would again be over capacity.

Initial construction of the southern bypass will be a two lane limited controlled access facility with 60 m (200 ft) of right-of-way. As traffic demand increases the facility can be upgraded to a four lane cross section. Also, proposed in connection with the construction of the NC 24-27 bypass is widening of NC 22 to a four lane facility from the southern Carthage Planning Boundary to the NC 24-27 Bypass. An interchange would also be constructed to tie the bypass to NC 22. Portions of existing US 15-501 between Vass Road and NC 22 would be used as a local route.

Vass Road (SR 1802) - Traffic is well below capacity on this two lane facility between US 15-501 and Monroe Street (NC 24-27) in Carthage. Its current width should be adequate in the design year.

Vass-Carthage Road (SR 1803) - This road is a two lane, 6.10 meters (20 ft) wide thoroughfare connecting the south eastern planning boundary to US 15-501 and Vass Road (SR 1802). It is recommended that this facility be widened to a 6.70 meters (22 ft) cross-section.

Niagra-Carthage Road (SR 1802) - This two lane route has a mix of residential and industrial development. The existing traffic volume is 1100 vpd (vehicles per day) and the projected traffic volume for the year 2025 is 2000 vpd. With the current pavement width of 5.49 meters (18 ft) and the future volume it is recommended that the pavement be widened to 6.70 meters (22 ft) as a safety improvement.

Glendon-Carthage Road (SR 1006) - SR 1006 travels between NC 24-27 and the northern planning boundary. This two lane facility has a 6.70 meters (20 ft) width and no improvements are currently recommended.

Summit Street - This northern radial route connects the growing residential area to the Central Business District in Carthage. The existing cross section should be sufficient through the design year.

Old River Road (SR 1651) - This two lane facility connects Summit Street to Glendon-Carthage Road (SR 1006). This route is mostly residential but it also used as a cut through route from the Central Business District to Glendon-Carthage Road and destinations north of the planning area. No improvements are recommended at this time.

Old Glendon Road (SR 1644) - This facility in the northwest planning area is a two lane, 5.49 meter (18 ft) wide thoroughfare that serve mostly residential traffic. It is recommended as a safety improvement that this facility be widened to 6.70 meters (22 ft) from NC 22-24-27 to the existing 6.70 meters (22 ft) pavement on Old Glendon Road (SR 1644).

Bethlehem Church Road (SR 1261) - This two lane facility that is located in the western planning area connects into NC 22-24-27. This route is mostly residential. The existing cross section is adequate for the design period.

Dowd Road (SR 1240) - Currently this is a two lane radial from the southwest that connects into the traffic circle at McReynolds Street (NC 22-24-27). This route serves mostly residential traffic and no improvements are currently recommended.

Minor Thoroughfares

The roadways serving as minor thoroughfares main purpose is to collect traffic from local access streets and carry it to the major thoroughfares.

Saunders Street - Currently this is a minor two lane facility in the central business district that serves primarily commercial traffic. It is recommended that this facility be converted from a existing two lane, two directional facility to a two lane, one-way facility. This facility would the eastern direction of the proposed one-way pair from Ray Street to Vass Road (SR 1802).

Ray Street - This minor thoroughfare connects Barrett Street to Saunders Street. It is recommended that this facility become the western portion of the proposed one-way pair.

Barrett Street - This minor two lane facility is recommended to become the other portion of the proposed one-way pair. This facility will need to be widen to cross section J to accommodate the future traffic demands. Also it is recommended that the section of Barrett Street at the NC 24-27 intersection be realigned to provide better access and transition to the one-way pair facility.

Rockingham Street - This minor radial connects McNeil Street (NC 22) to Monroe Street (NC 24-27). This is mostly a residential area with the Carthage Elementary and Middle School located along Rockingham Street. No improvements are recommended for this two-lane facility.

Cornell Road (SR 1256) - This route in the southern part of the planning area connects Dowd Road (SR 1240) to NC 22. This route is mostly residential. The existing cross section of Cornell Road should be sufficient through the design year.

Priest Hill Road (SR 1653) - This route in the north-eastern part of the planning area connects US 15-501 to Old River Road (SR 1651). This route is mostly residential. The existing cross section of Priest Hill Road should be sufficient through the design year.

Chapter 3

Implementation of the Thoroughfare Plan

nce the thoroughfare plan has been developed and adopted, implementation is one of th
nportant aspects of the transportation plan. Unless implementation is an integral part of
·ocess,. the effort and expense associated with developing the plan is lost. There are sev
/ailable for use by the Town of Carthage to assist in the implementation of the thorough
hey are described in detail in this Chapter.

:tate-Municipal Adoption of the Thoroughfare Plan

he Town of Carthage and the North Carolina Department of Transportation have mutua
)proved the thoroughfare plan shown in Figure 2. This mutually approved plan serve a~
ir the Department of Transportation in the development of the road and highway system
arthage. The approval of the plan by the Town enables standard road regulations and la
)ntrols to be used effectively in the. implementation of this plan. As part of the plan, the
1d Department of Transportation shall reach agreement on the responsibilities for existi1
:oposed streets and highways. Facilities which are designated as State responsibility wi
)nstructed and maintained by the Division of Highways. Facilities which are designatec
1unicipal responsibility will be constructed and maintained by the municipality.

:ubdivision Controls

ubdivision regulations require every subdivider to submit to the Town Planning Board a
1y proposed subdivision. It also requires that subdivisions be constructed to certain star
hrough this process, it is possible to require the subdivision streets do conform to the
1oroughfare plan and to reserve or protect necessary right-of-way for projected roads an·
ighways that are to become a part of the thoroughfare plan. The construction of subdivi
reets ·to adequate standards ·reduces maintenance costs and simplifies the transfer of stre
tate Highway System. Appendix C outlines the recommended subdivision design stand
1ey pertain to road construction.

..and Use Controls

.and use regulations are an important tool in that they regulate future land development ;
1inimize undesirable development along roads and highways. The land use regulatory s
an improve highway safety by requiring sufficient setbacks to provide for adequate sigh
istances and by requiring off-street parking.

)evelopment Reviews

)riveway access· to a state-maintained street or highway is reviewed by the District Engi1
ffice and by the Traffic Engineering Branch of the North Carolina Department of Trans)
1 addition, any development expected to generate large volumes of traffic (e.g., shoppin
ast food restaurants, or large industries) may be comprehensively studied by staff from t
:ngineering Branch, Planning and Environmental Branch, and/or Roadway Design Unit
JCDOT. If done at an early stage, it is often possible to significantly improve the devel(
ccessibility while preserving the integrity of the thoroughfare plan.

Funding Sources

Capital Improvements Program

A capital improvement program makes it easier to build a planned thoroughfare system. A capital improvement program consists of two lists of projects. The first is a list of highway projects that are designated as a municipal responsibility and are to be implemented with municipal funds. The second is a list of local projects designated as State responsibility to be included in the Transportation Improvement Program.

Transportation Improvement Program

North Carolina's Transportation Improvement Program (TIP) is a document which lists all major construction projects the Department of Transportation plans for the next seven years. Similar to local Capital Improvement Program projects, TIP projects are matched with projected funding sources. Each year when the TIP is updated, completed projects are removed, programed projects are advanced, and new projects are added.

During annual TIP public hearings, municipalities request projects to be included in the TIP. A Board of Transportation member reviews all of the project requests in a particular area of the state. Based on the technical feasibility, need, and available funding, the board member decides which projects will be included in the TIP. In addition to highway construction and widening, TIP funds are available for bridge replacement projects, highway safety projects, public transit projects, railroad projects, and bicycle projects.

Industrial Access Funds

If an Industry wishes to develop property that does not have access to a state maintained highway and certain economic conditions are met, then funds may be made available for construction of an access road.

Small Urban Funds

Small Urban funds are annual discretionary funds made to municipalities with qualifying projects. The maximum amount is $1,000,000 per year per division. A town may have multiple projects. Requests for Small Urban Fund assistance should be directed to the appropriate Board of Transportation member and Division Engineer.

The North Carolina Highway Trust Fund Law

The Highway Trust Fund Law was established in 1989 as a plan with four major goals for North Carolina's roads and highways. These goals are:

1. To complete the remaining 1,716 miles of four lane construction on the 3,600 mile North Carolina Intrastate System.

2. To construct a multilane connector in Asheville and portions of multilane loops in Charlotte, Durham, Greensboro, Raleigh, Wilmington, and Winston-Salem.

3. To supplement the secondary roads appropriation in order to pave, by 1999, 10,000 miles of unpaved secondary roads carrying 50 or more vehicles per day, and all other unpaved secondary roads by 2006.

4. To supplement the Powell Bill Program.

ion of this bill which will benefit Carthage, over the thirty year planning period, is the
f most, if not all, of its unpaved roads on the State maintained system. Also, there will be
ease in Carthage Powell Bill Funds if these newly paved roads are in the Carthage
te Limits. For more information on the Highway Trust Fund Law, contact the Program
ment Branch of the North Carolina Department to Transportation.

ementation Recommendations

owing table provides a break down of the projects recommended in the Carthage
hfare Plan and the corresponding method that would best suit the implementation of the
oject.

Table 1

ts	Funding Sources				Methods of Implementation			
	Local Funds	TIP Funds	Indust. Access	Small Urban	T-fare Plan	Subdiv. Ord.	Zoning Ord.	Development Review

* Widen from a two-lane to a three-lane cross section between McNeill Street and Vass Road.

struction Priorities and Cost Estimates

iction priorities will vary depending on what criteria are considered and what weight is
d to the various criteria. Most people would agree that improvements to the major
ghfare system and major traffic routes would be more important than minor thoroughfares
traffic volumes are lower. To be in the North Carolina Transportation Improvement
m, a project must show favorable benefits relative to costs and should not be prohibitively
ive to the environment. The potential cost estimate of three Carthage projects with respect
iser benefits, and the probabilities that economic development will be stimulated and
imental impact will be minimized are given in Table 3.A guide to this table is shown in
).

Table 2

Probability Estimation Guide	
Subjective Evaluation	Impact Probability
Excellent - very substantial	1.00
Very good - substantial	0.75
Good -considerable	0.50
Fair - some	0.25
Poor - none	0.00

Reduced road user cost should result from any roadway improvement, from a simple widenin; the construction of a new roadway. Roadway improvements should also relieve congested or unsafe conditions. Comparisons of the existing and the proposed facilities have been made in terms of vehicle operating costs, travel time costs, and accident costs. These user benefits are computed as total dollar savings over the 30 year design period using data such as project len; base year and design year traffic volumes, traffic speed, type of facility, and volume/capacity ratio.

The impact of a project on economic development potential is shown as the probability that it stimulate the economic development of an area by providing access to developable land and reducing transportation costs. It is a subjective estimate based on the knowledge of the propo project, local development characteristics, and land development potential. The probability is rated on a scale from 0 (representing no development potential) to 1.00 (representing excellen development potential).

The environmental impact analysis considers the effect of a project on the physical, social/cul and economic environment. Below are listed the thirteen items that are considered when evaluating the impacts on the environment.

* air quality   * educational facilities

* water resources   * churches

* soils and geology   * parks and recreational facilities

* wildlife   * historic sites and landmarks

* vegetation   * public health and safety

* neighborhoods   * aesthetics

* noise

The environmental impact analysis also uses a probability rating from 0 representing no ben the environment) to 1.00 (representing a positive impact to the environment). A negative val assigned to the probability to indicate a negative impact. The summation of both positive an negative impact probabilities with respect to these factors provides a measure of the relative environmental impacts of a project. Table 2 shows the probability scale used in the analysis. table can be used as a guideline for interpreting the "Economic Development" and Environm Impact" values given in Table 3.

Table 3

* Widen from a two-lane to a three-lane cross section between McNeil Street and Vass Road.

14

at would be derived from any project is the cost of its construction. A
iigh projected benefits, might prove to be unjustified due to the excessive
.ction. The highway costs estimated in this report are based on the
uction costs for similar project types. The anticipated right-of-way costs
:rage cost per acre for property throughout the Carthage Planning Area
ve project. Table 4 provides a break down of total project cost into
ht-of-way cost for the major project proposals for the Thoroughfare Plan.

Table 4

tential Project Cost Estimates for Major Projects

Construction Cost	Right-of-way Cost	Total Cost
2,460,000	330,000	2,790,000
15,930,000	1,410,000	17,340,000
125,000	N/A	125,000

nalysis Town of Carthage's Roadway System

sent an analysis of the ability of the existing street system to serve the area's travel
sis is placed not only on detecting the deficiencies, but on understanding their
eficiencies may be localized and the result of substandard highway design,
ment width, or intersection controls. Alternately, the underlying problem may be
tem deficiency such as a need for a bypass, loop facility, construction of missing
nal radials.

ravel Patterns

he roadway system must first look at existing travel patterns and identify existing
his includes roadway capacity and safety analysis. Also in an urban area, a street's
traffic is generally controlled by the spacing of major intersections, access control,
ent, and the traffic control devices (such as signals) utilized.

g picture of travel in the area has been developed, the engineer must analyze
impact the future system. These factors include forecasted population growth,
opment potential, and land use trends. This information will be used to determine
ies in the transportation system.

nalysis of the Existing System

if the adequacy of the existing street system is a comparison of traffic volumes
ty of the streets to move traffic freely at a desirable speed. The ability of a street to
:ely, safely, and efficiently with a minimum delay is controlled primarily by the
or devices utilized. Thus, the ability of a street to move traffic can be increased by
ing and turning movements, using proper sign and signal devices, and by the
other traffic engineering strategies.

maximum number of vehicles which has a "reasonable expectation" of passing
ction of a roadway, during a given time period under prevailing roadway and
ns. The relationship of traffic volumes to the capacity of the roadway will
evel of service (LOS) being provided. Six levels of service have been selected for
ies. They are given letter designations from A to F with LOS A representing the
conditions and LOS F the worst.

of service are illustrated in Figure 3, and they are defined on the following pages.
: are general and conceptual in nature, but may be applied to urban arterial levels of
s of service for interrupted flow facilities vary widely in terms of both the user's
ervice quality and the operational variables used to describe them. The 1995
city Manual contains more detailed descriptions of the levels of service as defined
y type.

Level of Service

LOS A

Describes primarily free flow conditions. The motorist experiences a high level of physical and psychological comfort. The effects of minor incidents or breakdowns are easily absorbed. Even at the maximum density, the average spacing between vehicles is about 528 ft, or 26 car lengths.

LOS B

Represents reasonably free flow conditions. The ability to maneuver within the traffic stream is only slightly restricted. The lowest average spacing between vehicles is about 330 ft, or 18 car length.

LOS C

Provides for stable operations, but flows approach the range in which small increases will cause substantial deterioration in service. Freedom to maneuver is noticeably restricted. Minor incidents may still be absorbed, but the local decline in service will be great. Queues may be expected to form behind any significant blockage. Minimum average spacings are in the range of 220 ft, or 11 car lengths.

LOS D

Borders on unstable flow. Density begins to deteriorate somewhat more quickly with increasing flow. Small increases in flow can cause substantial deterioration in service. Freedom to maneuver is severely limited, and the driver experiences drastically reduced comfort levels. Minor incidents can be expected to create substantial queuing. At the limit, vehicles are spaced at about 165 ft, or nine car lengths.

LOS E

Describes operation at **capacity.** Operations at this level are extremely unstable, because there are virtually no usable gaps in the traffic stream. Any disruption to the traffic stream, such as a vehicle entering from a ramp, or changing lanes, requires the following vehicles to give way to admit the vehicle. This can establishes a disruption wave that propagates through the upstream traffic flow. At capacity, the traffic stream has no ability to dissipate any disruption. Any incident can be expected to produce a serious breakdown with extensive queuing. Vehicles are spaced at approximately six car lengths, leaving little room to maneuver.

LOS F

Describes forced or breakdown flow. Such conditions generally exist within queues forming behind breakdown points.

LOS D.

LOS E.

LOS F.

F SERVICE   FIGURE 3

Traffic Accidents

Traffic accident are often used as an indicator for locating congestion problems. Traffic accident records can also be reviewed to identify problem locations or deficiencies such as poor design, inadequate signing, ineffective parking, or poor sight distance. Accident patterns developed from analysis of accident data can lead to improvements that will reduce the number of accidents.

Table 6 is a summary of the accidents occurring in Carthage between January 1992 and December 1994. This table only includes locations with 5 or more accidents. The "Total" column indicates the total number of accidents reported within 200 ft (61.0 m) of the intersection during the study period indicated. The severity listed is the average accident severity for that location.

Table 5

Location with 5 or More Accidents in a 3-Year Period

Locations	Angle	Rear End	Ran Off Road	Left Turn	Right Turn	Other	Total	Severity
US 15-501/NC 22		2		2		2	6	2.23
US 15-501/NC 24-27	1	4	5				10	7.66
US 15-501/SR 1833		7					7	5.23

Both the severity and number of accidents should be considered when investigating accident data. The severity of every accident is measured with a series of weighting factors developed by NCDOT's Division of Highways. In terms of these factors, a fatal or incapacitating accident is 47.7 times more severe than one involving only property damage, and an accident resulting in minor injury is 11.8 times more severe than one with only property damage. To request a more detailed accident analysis for any of the above mentioned intersection, or other intersections of concern, the Town should contact the Division 8 Traffic Engineer.

1995 Traffic Capacity Analysis

Capacity Deficiencies - Figure 4 depicts the base year (1995) major street system, and the **ADT** (Average Daily Traffic). A comparison of the base year ADT to capacities reveals several streets near or over practical capacity (LOS D). These areas are highlighted, and include:

Monroe Street (NC 24-27) - From the eastern planning boundary to the traffic circle is currently near capacity. The capacity on this section is 13,000 vpd (vehicles per day). Currently approximately 12,000 vpd are using the section between McNeill Street (NC 22) and the traffic circle in downtown Carthage. By the year 2025, if no improvements are made to the existing system, this volumes is expected to increase to 19,900 vpd.

McReynolds Street (NC 22-24-27) - From the traffic circle to the western planning boundary has a capacity of 13,000 vpd in the central business district. The capacity of the facility in areas outside the CBD is 12,000 vpd. In 1995 the average daily traffic volume was 8,500 vpd. By the year 2025 volumes are expected to increase to 15,000 vpd.

21

US 15-501 & NC 22 - From the southern planning boundary to thè US 15-501, NC 22 intersection has a capacity of 13,000 vpd. In 1994 the average daily traffic volume was 10,000 vpd. By the year 2025 volumes are expected to increase to 15,300 vpd.

No Build Alternative - Not implementing a thoroughfare plan or elements of it could be called a No-Build Alternative. This means that there would be no new construction or roadway improvements to the Carthage Thoroughfare system except for routine maintenance. If no improvements are made to NC 24-27 and a Bypass is not constructed during the planning period, the increased traffic volumes and normal growth will result in a dramatic reduction in transportation quality. The LOS on NC 24-27 will drop to LOS E. At LOS E the operating speed will drop significantly, and the queues of traffic currently experienced behind slow moving vehicles will get considerably longer. The absence of improvements will negatively impact growth and business in the Carthage area. Figure 5 shows the existing system assuming that no improvement are made by the design year.

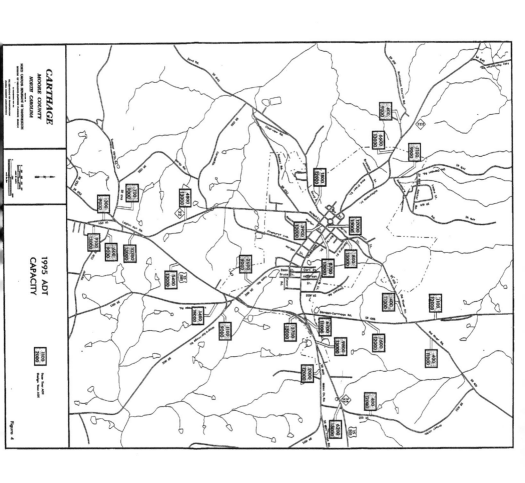

CARTHAGE
MOORE COUNTY
NORTH CAROLINA

1995 ADT
CAPACITY

Figure 4

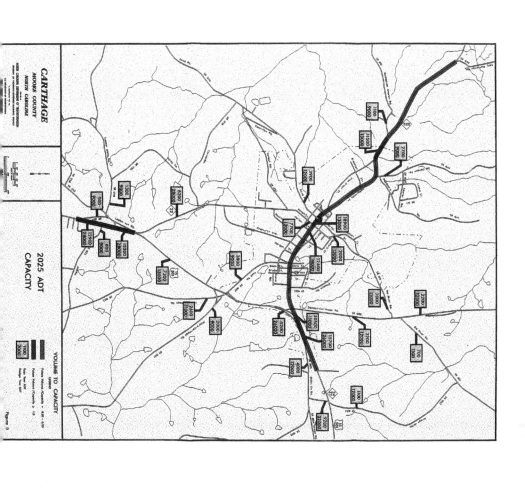

CARTHAGE
MOORE COUNTY
NORTH CAROLINA

NORTH CAROLINA DEPARTMENT OF TRANSPORTATION

2025 ADT
CAPACITY

VOLUME TO CAPACITY

Figure 5.

Chapter 5

Population, Land Use, and Traffic

Factors Affecting the Future Roadway System

The objective of thoroughfare planning is to develop a transportation system that will meet future travel demand and enable people and goods to travel safely and economically. To determine the needs of an area it is important to understand the role of population, economics, and land use have on the highway system. Examination of these factors helps to explain historic travel patterns and lays the groundwork for thoroughfare planning.

In order to formulate an adequate year 2025 thoroughfare plan, reliable forecasts of future travel characteristics must be achieved. The factors of population, vehicle usage trends, economy and land use play a significant role in determining the transportation needs of the area, and must be carefully analyzed. Additional items may include the effects of legal controls such as subdivision regulations and zoning ordinances, availability of public utilities and physical features of the area.

The first step in the development of the thoroughfare plan is to define the planning period and the planning area. The planning period is typically on the order of 30 years. The base year for the Carthage study was 1994, and the year 2025 was chosen to be the end point of the study period (31 years). The planning area is generally the limits to which urbanization is expected to occur during the planning period. The planning area is then subdivided into traffic analysis zones. Figure 6 shows the planning area boundary and zones.

Population

The amount of traffic on a section of roadway is a function of the size and location of the population which it serves. Investigating past trends in population growth and forecasting future population growth and dispersion is one of the first steps for a transportation planner. Table 6 shows the historical and projected population trends for Carthage through 2025. A graphical illustration of the population is shown in Figure 7.

Table 6

1970	1,034	39,048	4,640
1980	925	50,505	5,241
1990	976	59,000	4,837
1994	1,375	66,151	5,292c
2000	1,427d	70,360a	5,488c
2010	1,487d	75,275a	5,721c
2020	1,528d	79,419a	5,877c
2025	1,542d	82,386b	5,932c

a/Estimate by Office State Budget and Management
b/Projection based on past trends
c/Estimated County Population x Township % of County
d/Estimated Township population X Carthage % of Township

The most important population estimate for development of the thoroughfare plan is that of the planning area. Even though government census data is not available for the transportation planning area, other methods of estimation of population are available. The 1994 housing "windshield" survey for this study area gave a final count of 1000 homes inside the Carthage Planning Area. The housing count was then multiplied by the average persons per dwelling unit for planning area (2.54), to give a total planning area population of 2,540. Population projections are shown in Table 7.

Table 7

Carthage Population Forecasts

Year	Population
1994	2,540
2000	2,620
2010	2,760
2020	2,910
2025	2,990

Economy and Employment

One of the more important factors to be considered in estimating the future traffic growth of an area is its economic base. The number of employers and the employee's income or purchasing power influences how much population can be supported in the area and the number of motor vehicles that will be locally owned and operated. Generally, as the family income increases so does the number of vehicles owned, as well as the number of vehicles trips generated per day by each household. An accurate projection of the future economy of the area is essential to estimating future travel demand.

Factors which will influence economic growth and development in Carthage over the 30 year planning period is development along the US 15-501 and NC 22 corridors in the Carthage Planning Area. The working population of Carthage is mainly a mixture of industrial, service, and office industries. These three types of employment, employ over 75% of the working population of Carthage. Table 8 Employment Break Down for Carthage was developed using the sum of the estimated jobs of each employer for 1994.

Table 8

Employment Break Down for Carthage

Type of Employment	Employment 1994	Employment 2025
Industrial	532	612
Retail	301	350
Highway Retail	142	175
Office	442	525
Service	441	525
Total	1858	2187

Land Use

Land use refers to the physical patterns of activities and functions within a city or county. Nearly all traffic problems in a given area can attributed in some form to the type of land use. For example, a large industrial plant might be the cause of congestion during shift change hours as its workers come and go. However, during the remainder of the day few problems, if any, may occur. The spatial distribution of different types of land use is the predominant determinant of when, where, and why congestion occurs. The attraction between different land uses and their association with travel varies depending on the size, type, intensity, and spatial separation of each.

For use in transportation planning, land uses are grouped into four categories:

1. Residential - all land devoted to the housing of people (excludes hotels and motels)

2. Commercial - all land devoted to retail trade including consumer and business services and offices

3. Industrial - all land devoted to manufacturing, storage, warehousing, and transportation of products

4. Public -all land devoted to social, religious, educational, cultural, and political activities.

Figure 8 shows the planning area's existing land use.

Anticipated future land use is a logical extension of the present spatial distribution. Determination of where expected growth is to occur within the planning area facilitates the location of proposed thoroughfares or the improvements of existing thoroughfares. Areas of anticipated development and growth for Carthage are:

1. Residential - A large amount of Carthage's residential land development is located in the southern and the north western portions of the planning area. The potential for new residential development also can be found in the western section of the planning area.

2. Commercial/Retail - Most of the commercial development, in Carthage is on Monroe and McReynold Street (NC 24-27) or McNeill Street (NC 22) so it is anticipated that this development will continue in the future.

3. Industrial - The industrial development in Carthage is located in the southeastern portion of the planning area. This development is mainly on Niagra-Carthage Road (SR 1802) and it is anticipated that this area and US 15-501 will continue to develop in the future.

4. Public - The Town of Carthage has no public areas now but a recreation park is being planned in the southern planning area along US 15-501.

The western and southern portions of the planning area have the largest growth expectations. Hopefully, the implementation of the thoroughfare plan and NC 24-27 Bypass will help alleviate an traffic congestion due to this new development.

Future Travel Demand

Travel demand is generally reported in average daily traffic counts. Traffic counts are taken regularly in and around Carthage by the North Carolina Department of Transportation. To estimate future travel demand, traffic trends over the past twenty years were studied. A comparison of annual growth rates from 1970 to 1994 at various count locations in Carthage shows the average annual growth rates ranging from 1.0% to 7.0%. The largest growth was noted on lower volume roads, where a given increase will result in a higher percentage. Figures 4 and 5 shows existing and expected traffic volumes for the Carthage Planning Area. The introduction of new residential and commercial developments in the planning area will cause increases in traffic growth in those immediate areas. Eventually, this increase will level off and follow the growth pattern of the surrounding area.

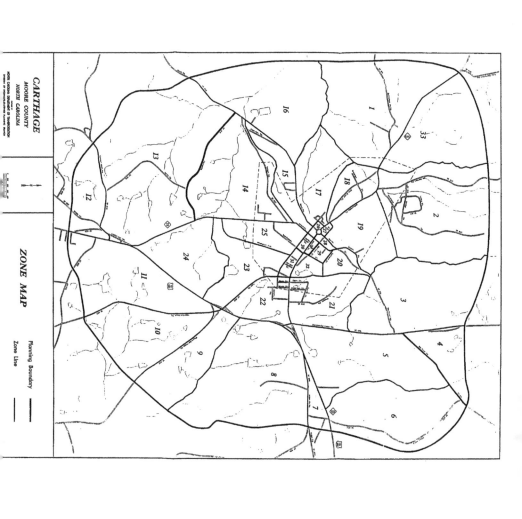

CARTHAGE

MOORE COUNTY
NORTH CAROLINA

NORTH CAROLINA DEPARTMENT OF TRANSPORTATION
DIVISION OF HIGHWAYS/DEPARTMENT PLANNING BRANCH

ZONE MAP

Planning Boundary ━━━━━

Zone Line ━━━━━

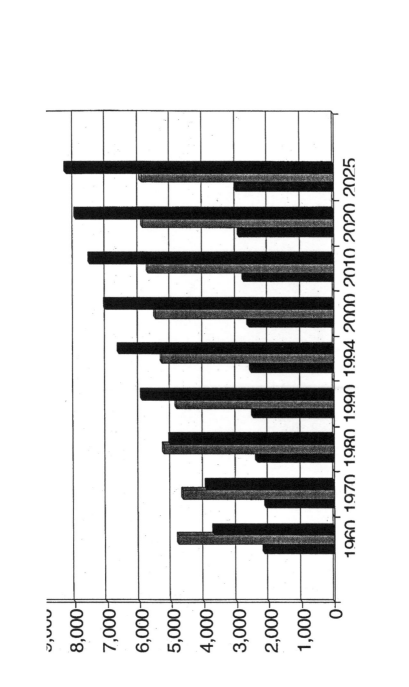

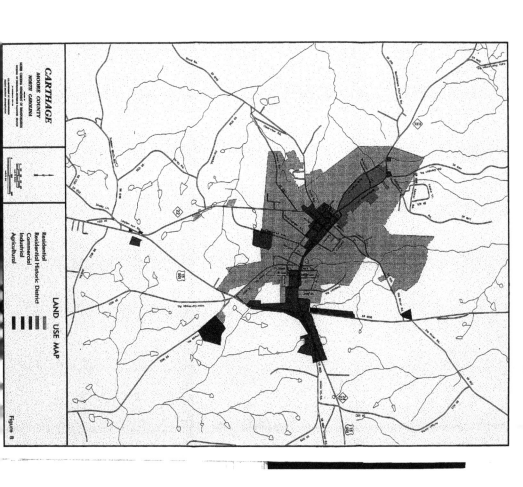

CARTHAGE
MOORE COUNTY
NORTH CAROLINA

LAND USE MAP

Residential
Residential Historic District
Commercial
Industrial
Agricultural

Figure 8

Chapter 6

Environmental Concerns

In the past several years, environmental considerations associated with highway construction have come to the forefront of the planning process. The legislation that dictates the necessary procedures regarding environmental impacts is the National Environmental Policy Act. Section 102 of this act requires the execution of an environmental impact statement, or EIS, for road projects that have a significant impact on the environment. Included in an EIS would be the project's impact on wetlands, water quality, historic properties, wildlife, and public lands. While this report does not cover the environmental concerns in as much detail as an EIS would, preliminary research was done on several of these factors and is included below.

Wetlands

In general terms, wetlands are lands where saturation with water is the dominant factor in determining the nature of soil development and the types of plant and animal communities living in the soil and on its surface. The single feature that most wetlands share is soil or substrata that is at least periodically saturated with or covered by water. Water creates severe physiological problems for all plants and animals except those that are adapted for life in it or in saturated soil.

Wetlands are crucial ecosystems in our environment. They help regulate and maintain the hydrology of our rivers, lakes, and streams by slowly storing and releasing flood waters. They help maintain the quality of our water by storing nutrients, reducing sediment loads, and reducing erosion. They are also critical to fish and wildlife populations. Wetlands provide an important habitat for about one third of the plant and animal species that are federally listed as threatened or endangered.

In this study, the impacts to wetland were determined using the National Wetlands Inventory Mapping, available from the U. S. Fish and Wildlife Service. The location of wetlands throughout Carthage are shown in Figure 9.

Wetland impacts have been avoided or minimized to the greatest extent possible while preserving the integrity of the transportation plan.

Threatened and Endangered Species

A preliminary review of the Federally Listed Threatened and Endangered Species within Carthage's Planning Area was done to determine the effects that new corridors could have on the wildlife. These species were identified using mapping from the North Carolina Department of Environment, Health, and Natural Resources.

The Threatened and Endangered Species Act of 1973 allows the U. S. Fish and Wildlife Service to impose measures on the Department of Transportation to mitigate the environmental impacts of a road project on endangered plants and animals and critical wildlife habitats. By locating rare species in the planning stage of road construction, we are able to avoid or minimize these impacts.

There was one state listed threatened or endangered species identified in the Carthage Planning Area. It is listed below. Detailed field investigation is recommended prior to construction of any highway project in this area.

Endangered Species:

Amorpha Georgiana Var Georgiana (Georgia Indigo Bush)

There were no other species identified in the Carthage Planning Area that are significantly rare or are of special concerns in North Carolina.

Historic Sites

The location of historic sites in Carthage was investigated to determine the possible impacts of the various projects studied. The federal government has issued guidelines requiring all State Transportation Departments to make special efforts to preserve historic sites. In addition, the State of North Carolina has issued its own guidelines for the preservation of historic sites. These two pieces of legislation are described below:

> **National Historic Preservation Act** - Section 106 of this act requires the Department of Transportation to identify historic properties listed in the National Register of Historic Places and properties eligible to be listed. The DOT must consider the impact of its road projects on these properties and consult with the Federal Advisory Council on Historic Preservation.

> **NC General Statute 121-12(a)** - This statute requires the DOT to identify historic properties listed on the National Register, but not necessarily those eligible to be listed. DOT must consider impacts and consult with the North Carolina Historical Commission, but it is not bound by their recommendations.

There are currently three properties in Carthage planning area that are listed on the National Register of Historic Places. There is also one property that is actively on the study list for the National Register. The following is a list of Historic Places on the National Register in the Carthage Planning Area and there locations are shown in Figure 9:

Historic Places

Moore County Courthouse (#1466)
Bruce-Dowd-Kennedy House (#700) (NC 22)
Carthage Historic District (#1664)
Alexander Hamilton McNeil House (Pinecrest Avenue) *

* Actively on the Study List.

None of these properties should be affected by the projects proposed on the thoroughfare plan. However, care should be taken to make certain that all historic sites and natural settings are preserved. Therefore, a closer study should be done in regard to the local historic sites prior to the construction of any proposal.

Archaeology

There were no significant archaeology sites located in the Carthage Planning Area. However, care should be taking to make sure that any possible archaeological sites should be looked at closer prior to the construction of any proposals.

Environmental Data for Carthage

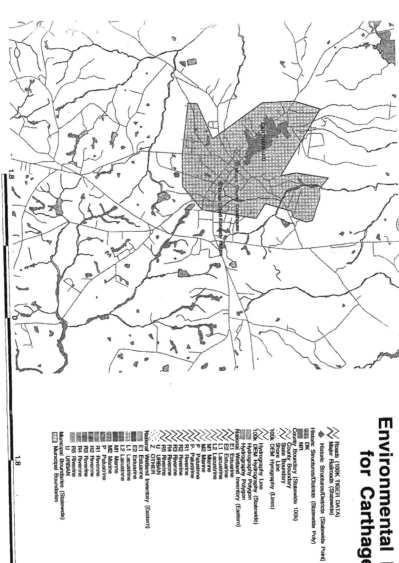

Carthage No

Maury County Courthouse

Frank David-Kinsey Tigner

N
W   E
S

1.8   0   1.8   3.6 Miles

Figure 9

Legend

Roads (100K TIGER DATA)
Major Railroads (Statewide)

Historic Structures/Districts (Statewide Point)
DK
NR

Historic Structures/Districts (Statewide Poly)
County Boundary (Statewide 100K)
State Line
Shore Line

100K DEM Hydrography (Lines)

Hydrography Line
100k DEM Hydrography (Statewide)
Hydrography Polygon
National Wetland Inventory (Eastern)
Hydrography Polygon

E1 Estuarine
L1 Lacustrine
L2 Lacustrine
M1 Marine
M2 Marine
P Palustrine
P Palustrine
R1 Riverine
R2 Riverine
R3 Riverine
R4 Riverine
R5 Riverine
U URBAN
Z OTHER

National Wetland Inventory (Eastern)

E1 Estuarine
E2 Estuarine
L1 Lacustrine
L2 Lacustrine
M1 Marine
M2 Marine
P Palustrine
R1 Riverine
R2 Riverine
R3 Riverine
R4 Riverine
R5 Riverine
U URBAN

Municipal Boundaries (Statewide)
Municipal Boundaries

Chapter 7

Traffic Model Development

In order to develop an efficient thoroughfare plan for the Town of Carthage it was necessary to develop and calibrate a traffic model of the Town. To develop a traffic model the following things are necessary: define the study area, collect traffic counts and socioeconomic data, determine the trip generation characteristics of the study area, calibrate the traffic model so that it duplicates patterns of the study area, and project socioeconomic data to the design year. Once the socioeconomic data has been projected the model may be used to evaluate various street system problems and alternate solutions to the problems.

The Study Area

The study area of Carthage consists of the Town and some additional outlaying areas (Figure 6). This area was divided into 34 zones for data collection and aggregation. These zones reflect similar land use throughout the planning area. The data for the dwelling units and employment for 1995 was collected from census data and windshield surveys. The projections of socioeconomic data to the future year was done based on past trends from previous census data and projections by the Office of State Planning.

The Base Year Network

The purpose of the traffic model is to replicate the conditions on the Town street system. Therefore it is necessary to represent the existing street system in the model. There is a balance between having too many streets on the model to allow it to be calibrated and not having enough streets to realistically duplicate existing conditions. Generally, all the major arterials and some of the major land access or collector streets need to be represented.

Street capacity is an important component of the model. The volume\capacity ratio (v\c) gives us our best indication of present and future traffic congestion.

Speed and distance are the major factors that define the minimum time paths from zone to zone. The model uses the minimum time paths as the basis for assigning traffic to streets. Generally in the Carthage model the speeds assigned to links of the street system are at or slightly below the posted speed limit. Figure 10 shows the Tranplan Network overlayed on the actual street system.

Data Requirements

In order to produce an adequate traffic model of the study area, two additional types of data are required. First, traffic counts on routes used in the model provide a basis for calibrating the model. These traffic counts show a snapshot of traffic conditions in the study area. Second, socioeconomic data (housing counts and employment estimates) are necessary in order to generate traffic for the model. The housing and socioeconomic data for the model are shown in Figures 13 and 14.

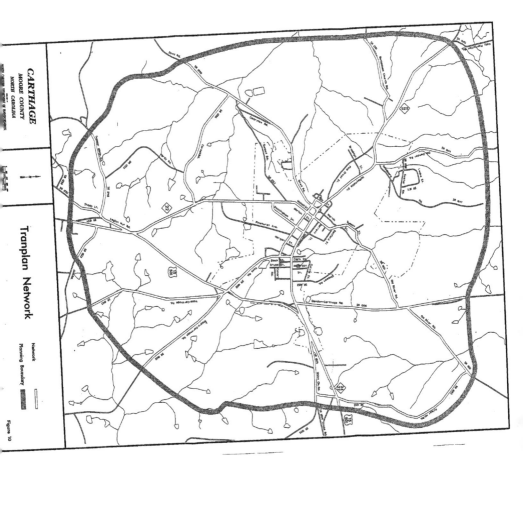

Tranplan Network

Network

Planning Boundary

Figure 10

Traffic Counts

The model must be calibrated against existing conditions in the study area. In order to calibrate the model traffic counts must be taken at various locations around the study area. The counts for much of the Carthage study were collected during September, 1994. Traffic count locations are found in Figure 11.

Also, volumes on all routes crossing the planning area boundary were counted. These counts show how much traffic is entering and exiting the study area.

Socioeconomic Data

The required data consists of a housing counts and employment estimates. The housing counts are used in the model as the generator of trips and employment is used as the attractor of trips.

The best indicator of the average number of trips made from a household income. Since there is no adequate method for determining household income, the type and quality of housing was used as an indicator of household income. The Statewide Planning staff conducted a windshield survey in October, 1994 to collect housing and employment data. The housing inventory was divided into five categories: excellent, above average, average, below average, and poor. Each of these categories was assigned a slightly different trip generation rate. Figure 12 shows the housing counts for each traffic zone.

The employment data that was collected was broken out by Standard Industrial Code classification and grouped into five categories: industry, special retail, retail, office and services. The number of employees of each business was estimated. This data was used with a regression equation developed from an origin and destination survey of a similar size Town to produce an attraction factor for each zone. Figure 13 shows total employment by traffic analysis zone.

Commercial Vehicles

Commercial vehicles have somewhat different trip generation characteristics than do privately owned vehicles. For the purposes of this model, and the little impact they were expected to have, commercial vehicles data was not collected.

Trip Generation

The trip generation process is the process by which external station volumes, housing data, and employment data are used to generate traffic volumes that duplicate the traffic volumes on the street network. The technical definition of a trip is slightly different then the definition of a trip used by the general public. Technically a trip only has one origin and one destination while the layman will often group, or chain, several short trips together as one longer trip.

Traffic inside the study area has three major components: through trips, internal-external trips, and internal trips. Through trips are produced outside the planning area and pass through enroute to a destination outside the planning area. Internal-external trips have one end of the trip outside of the planning area. Internal trips have both their origin and destination inside the planning area. For clarity the internal trips are further subdivided into trip purposes. The trip purposes for Carthage are home-based work, other-home based, and non-home based.

45

Through Trips

The Through Trip Table for this study was developed based on Technical Report 3 (Synthesized Through Trip Table for Small Urban Areas by Dr. David G. Modlin, Jr.).

Once these volumes were developed the Fratar balancing method was then used to balance the trip interchanges so that the total number of through trips at each external station is consistent with the total number of through trips at every other station. Generally five iterations are sufficient to balance the estimate between external zones.

External - Internal

The external-internal trip volume was determined by subtracting the through trip volume at each station from the total traffic volume at that station. See Table 11 for external-internal and through trip values.

Internal **Data Summary (IDS)**

IDS is the process that takes the external-internal traffic volumes, housing data, employment data, generation rates, and regression equations and generates the trip productions and trip attractions required by the gravity model. Housing units were stratified to account for differing trip generation rates for each classification. The individual trip generation rates give an average trip generation rate for the study area of 7.01 trips per dwelling unit (du) for 1994. This within the state average of 7 to 8 trips per dwelling unit. Trip attractions were produced using regression equations. The regression equations considers trip attractions to be related to the employment characteristics of the traffic zones. The regression equations for Carthage are:

$$OHB \quad Y = .10X_1 + 2.7X_2 + 5.5X_3 + 2.6X_4 + 1.2X_5$$
$$NHB \quad Y = .20X_1 + 2.7X_2 + 5.5X_3 + 2.6X_4 + 1.2X_5$$
$$EXT \quad Y = .50X_1 + 2.7X_2 + 5.5X_3 + 2.6X_4 + 1.2X_5$$

Where: Y = Attraction factor for each zone
X_1 = Industry (SIC codes 1-49)
X_2 = Retail (SIC codes 55, 58)
X_3 = Special Retail (SIC codes 50-54, 56, 57, 59)
X_4 = Office (SIC codes 60-67, 91-97)
X_5 = Services (SIC codes 70-76, 78-89, 99)

The output of the IDS program are trip productions and trip attractions for each zone divided into four trip purposes: home-based work, non-home based and external-internal. The trips are segregated into trip purposes because different trip lengths are associated with each trip purpose.

Internal Trip Distribution

Once the number of trips per traffic zone are determined, the trips must still be distributed to other traffic zones. The preferred method of distributing internal and external-internal trips, called the 'Gravity Model', states that the number of trips between Zone A and Zone B is proportional to the number of trips produced in Zone A multiplied by the number of trips attracted to Zone B multiplied by a travel time factor. The gravity model takes the form:

$$\cdot \text{ Sum } x=1,n \text{ of } A_x \, F_{t'x}$$

number of trips produced in zone i and attracted to zone j.
number of trips produced in zone i.
number of trips attracted to zone j.
travel time factor.
total number of zones.
origin zone number.
destination zone number.
zone number.

actor or friction factor (F) is critical to the gravity model distribution and must be
lly. The friction factor is dependent on the distance between the traffic zones and
ry to travel these distances. This factor is also dependent on the trip purpose. In
nis factor a gravity model calibration program is run with an initial friction factor
requency curve for each trip purpose. The initial friction factors used in the
were 100 for all trip purposes and time increments. Table 12 shows the actual
he friction factors and trip length frequency curves.

ration

traffic model is to predict the traffic on a street system at some future point in
f the model is not accurate, it is useless for this purpose. Therefore the model
ne existing traffic pattern. The actual calibration of the model is an iterative
incremental changes are made either in the trip generation, trip distribution, or
k. The purpose of each change is to allow the model to more accurately reflect
nditions upon which it is based. Only when the model can adequately reflect the
attern should it be used to predict traffic in the future. The model was calibrated
992 Average Daily Traffic Counts on all routes that it was available.

hecks

checks made on the model. The first is to follow trips through all the steps
model. The purpose of this check is to insure that no trips have been accidentally
racted from the model, and that no trips have been counted twice.

k is to compare the model generated trips on the screenlines with the ground
he screenlines. A model is considered to accurately reflect the overall patterns if
ates are from 95% to 105% of the ground counts on the screenlines. Table 9
ound counts with the model traffic volumes on the screenlines. Because of the
the EW screenline a higher amount of error was acceptable. See Figure 10 for
ons.

for the model is to match the traffic volumes on the links in the model with the
e location. The 'link counts' can be used to find particular places in the network
problems. Comparing the link counts with the ground counts for those links did
ignificant problems with the model.

47

Table 9

Actual vs Model Screenline Total

Screenline	Ground Count	Model Volume	Percent
A NS	13456	13270	1.01
B EW	5250	4250	1.24

Data Projections to the Design Year

In order to make use of the model the base year data must be modified to reflect assumed conditions in the design year. These projections and the previously developed regression equations were used to produce trip productions and attractions in the same manner as the base year.

Dwelling Unit Projections

Future dwelling units were determined by extending person per dwelling unit trends for Moore County linearly to the design year. The number of dwelling units are projected to increase by 8%. The Statewide Planning Unit projected residential growth and the Carthage Planning Board distributed these houses throughout the planning area. Figure 12 compares the classification of dwelling units in 1994 with the assumed classification in 2025.

Employment Projections

The Carthage Planning Board projected the employment to 2025 from the zones they anticipated employment growth. Those projections were added to the 1994 data. Employment projections throughout the planning area indicates slow, but steady, growth. Figure 13 compares the classification of employment data in 1994 with the assumed classification in 2025.

External and Through Trips

For the design year, external and through trips were projected from the base year using a linear projection of the past growth rate at each external station. Cordon Station Data can be found in Table 13.

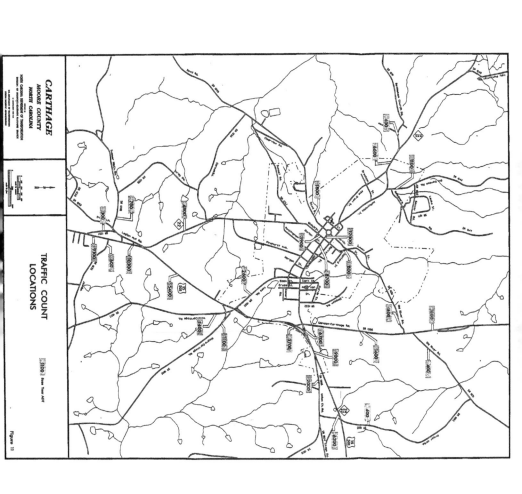

CARTHAGE
MOORE COUNTY
NORTH CAROLINA

TRAFFIC COUNT
LOCATIONS

Figure 11

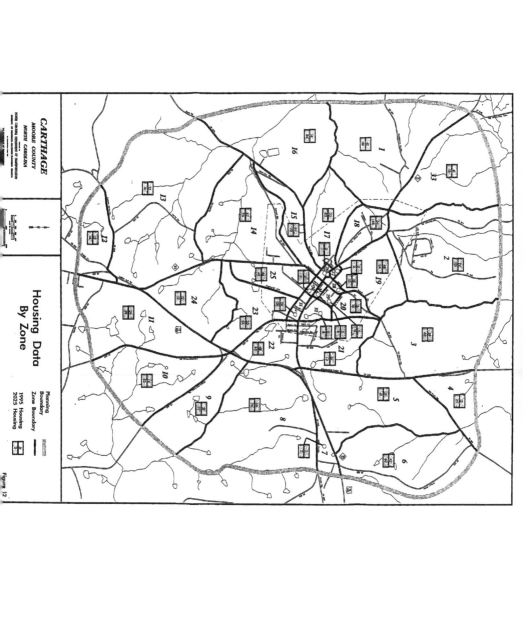

CARTHAGE
MOORE COUNTY
NORTH CAROLINA

Housing Data
By Zone

Planning
Boundary

Zone Boundary

1995 Housing
2025 Housing

Figure 12

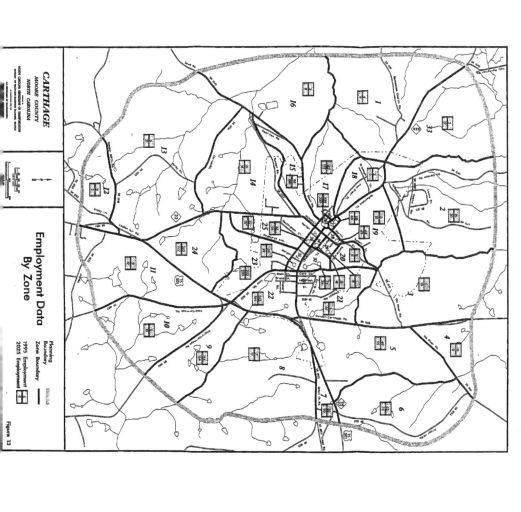

CARTHAGE
MOORE COUNTY
NORTH CAROLINA

NORTH CAROLINA DEPARTMENT OF TRANSPORTATION

Employment Data
By Zone

Planning
Boundary

Zone Boundary

1995 Employment
2025 Employment

Figure 13

Table 10

Year	Person/DU	Persons/Veh
1995	2.54	1.20
2025	2.35	1.04

X Usage Factor X $\dfrac{2025 \text{ Person/DU}}{1995 \text{ Person/DU}}$

ites

p Rate X Composite Factor - Average 1995 Trip Rate

$.40$ (7.01 X 1.05) - 7.01 = 0.36

───

nent

Trips - Ext-Int Trips Garaged Inside Planning Area X 0.40*

0 - 1,051) X 0.40 = 5,596

2 - 1,420) X 0.40 = 9,641

se and total of non-home based trips generated externally

vay external-internal trip by vehicles garaged outside the planning

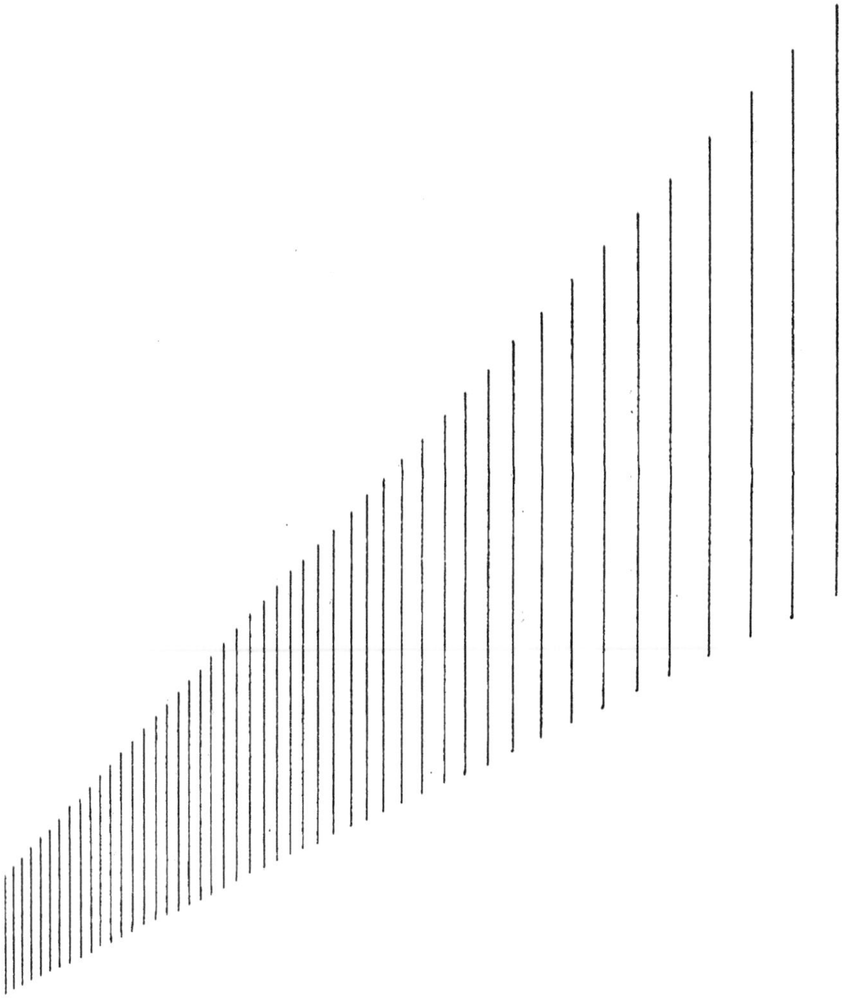

Appendix A

roughfare Planning Principles

o thoroughfare planning, but the primary mission is to assure that the
ively developed to serve future travel desires. Thus, the main
planning is to make provisions for street and highway
the need arises, feasible opportunities to make improvements exist.

ghfare Planning

derived from thoroughfare planning. First, each road or highway can
cific function and provide a specific level of service. This permits
truction, and maintenance costs. It also protects residential
es stability in travel and land use patterns. Second, local officials are
ents and can incorporate them into planning and policy decisions.
o design subdivisions in a non-conflicting manner, direct school and
their facilities, and minimize the damage to property values and
s sometimes associated with roadway improvements.

ssification Systems

functions, traffic service and land access, which when combined, are
conflict is not serious if both traffic and land service demands are
volumes are high, conflicts created by uncontrolled and intensely
lead to intolerable traffic flow friction and congestion.

ne thoroughfare plan is that it provides a functional system of streets
ins to destinations with directness, ease and safety. Different streets
and called on to perform specific functions, thus minimizing the traffic

an, elements are classified as major thoroughfares, minor
ss streets.

' traffic arteries of the urban area and they accommodate traffic
and through the area.

his type collect traffic from the local access streets and carry it to the

Local Access Streets

This classification covers streets that have a primary purpose of providing access to the abutting property. This classification may be further classified as either residential, commercial and/or industrial depending upon the type of land use that they serve.

Idealized Major Thoroughfare System

The coordinated system of major thoroughfares that is most adaptable to the desired lines of travel within an urban area and that is reflected in most urban area thoroughfare plans is the radial-loop system. The radial-loop system includes radials, crosstowns, loops, and bypasses (Figure A-1).

Radial streets provide for traffic movement between points located on the outskirts of the city and the central area. This is a major traffic movement in most cities, and the economic strength of the central business district depends upon the adequacy of this type of thoroughfare.

If all radial streets crossed in the central area, an intolerable congestion problem would result. To avoid this problem, it is very important to have a system of crosstown streets that form a loop around the central business district. This system allows traffic moving from origins on one side of the central area to destinations on the other side to follow the area's border. It also allows central area traffic to circle and then enter the area near a given destination. The effect of a good crosstown system is to free the central area of crosstown traffic, thus permitting the central area to function more adequately in its role as a business or pedestrian shopping area.

Loop system streets move traffic between suburban areas of the city. Although a loop may completely encircle the city, a typical trip may be from an origin near a radial thoroughfare to a destination near another radial thoroughfare. Loop streets do not necessarily carry heavy volumes of traffic, but they function to help relieve central areas. There may be one or more loops, depending on the size of the urban area. They are generally spaced one-half mile to one mile apart, depending on the intensity of land use.

A bypass is designed to carry traffic through or around the urban area, thus providing relief to the city street system by removing traffic that has no desire to be in the city. Bypasses are usually designed to through-highway standards, with control of access. Occasionally, a bypass with low traffic volume can be designed to function as a portion of an urban loop. The general effect of bypasses is to expedite the movement of through traffic and to improve traffic conditions within the city. By freeing the local streets for use by shopping and home-to-work traffic, bypasses tend to increase the economic vitality of the local area.

Objectives of Thoroughfare Planning

Thoroughfare planning is the process public officials use to assure the development of the most appropriate street system that will meet existing and future travel desires within the urban area. The primary aim of a thoroughfare plan is to guide the development of the urban street system in manner consistent with the changing traffic patterns. A thoroughfare plan will enable street improvements to be made as traffic demands increase, and it helps eliminate unnecessary improvements, so needless expense can be averted. By developing the urban street system to keep pace with increasing traffic demands, a maximum utilization of the system can be attained, requiring a minimum amount of land for street purposes. In addition to providing for traffic need the thoroughfare plan should embody those details of good urban planning necessary to present a pleasing and efficient urban community. The location of present and future population, commercial and industrial development affects major street and highway locations. Conversely,

thin the urban area will influence the urban

nclude: ˙

nt of an adequate major street system as land

sts;

rovements to the public through the coordination of

r actions, improvements, and development with full

ient of people and businesses through long range
rovements;

h as air pollution, resulting from transportation, and

ving both the operational efficiency of thoroughfares,
system coordination and layout.

by increasing the capability of the street to carry
f vehicular traffic, a street's capacity is defined by
pass a given point on a roadway during a given time
conditions. Capacity is affected by the physical
weather.

icity include:

et from two to four lanes more than doubles the
litional maneuverability for traffic.

ing the turning radii, adding exclusive turn lanes, and
the capacity of an existing intersection.

lignment -reduces the congestion caused by slow

luces side friction and improves a driver's field of

city include:

complete access control can often carry three times the
cess street with identical lane width and number.

* **Parking removal** -- Increases capacity by providing additional street width for traffic flow and reducing friction to flow caused by parking and unparking vehicles.

* **One-way operation** -- The capacity of a street can sometimes be increased 20-50%, depending upon turning movements and overall street width, by initiating one-way traffic operations. One-way streets can also improve traffic flow by decreasing potential traffic conflicts and simplifying traffic signal coordination.

* **Reversible lane** -- Reversible traffic lanes may be used to increase street capacity in situations where heavy directional flows occur during peak periods.

* **Signal phasing and coordination** -- Uncoordinated signals and poor signal phasing restrict traffic flow by creating excessive stop-and-go operation.

Altering travel demand is a third way to improve the efficiency of existing streets. Travel demand can be reduced or altered in the following ways:

* **Carpools** - Encourage people to form carpools and vanpools for journeys to work and other trip purposes. This reduces the number of vehicles on the roadway and raises the people carrying capability of the street system.

* **Alternate mode** - Encourage the use of transit and bicycle modes.

* **Work hours** - Encourage industries, businesses, and institutions to stagger work hours or establish variable work hours for employees. This will spread peak travel over a longer time period and thus reduce peak hour demand.

* **Land use** - Plan and encourage land use development or redevelopment in a more travel efficient manner.

System Efficiency

Another means for altering travel demand is the development of a more efficient system of streets that will better serve travel desires. A more efficient system can reduce travel distances, time, and cost to the user. Improvements in system efficiency can be achieved through the concept of functional classification of streets and development of a coordinated major street system.

Application of Thoroughfare Planning Principles

The concepts presented in the discussion of operational efficiency, system efficiency, functional classification, and idealized major thoroughfare system are the conceptual tools available to the transportation planner in developing a thoroughfare plan. In actual practice, thoroughfare planning is done for established urban area and is constrained by existing land use and street patterns, existing public attitudes and goals, and current expectations of future land use. Compromises must be made because of these and the many other factors that affect major street locations.

Through the thoroughfare planning process it is necessary from a practical viewpoint that certain basic principles be followed as closely as possible. These principles are listed below:

1. The plan should be derived from a thorough knowledge of today's travel - its component parts, and the factors that contribute to it, limit it, and modify it.

ust be sufficient to warrant the designation and development of each
:horoughfare plan should be designed to accommodate a large portion of
ments on a few streets.

onform to and provide for the land development plan for the area.

ions must be given to urban development beyond the current planning
ly in outlying or sparsely developed areas that have development
:ssary to designate thoroughfares on a long-range planning basis to
ay for future thoroughfare development.

stent with the above principles and realistic in terms of travel trends, the
omically feasible.

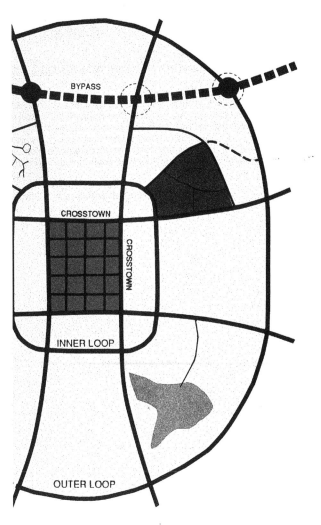

BYPASS

CROSSTOWN

CROSSTOWN

INNER LOOP

OUTER LOOP

PROPOSED

LAND USES

COMMERCIAL/BUSINESS

RESIDENTIAL

INDUSTRIAL

Appendix B

Street Tabulation and Recommendations

tabulation of all streets identified as elements of the Town of
table includes a description of each section, as well as the
-way for each section. Also included are existing and projected
dway capacity, and the recommended ultimate lane
raints, these recommended cross-sections are given in the form
description of each of these codes and a illustrative figure for

be helpful in interpreting the table:

ry

ry

ry

Appendix B
Thoroughfare Plan Street Tabulation and Recomm

			PRACTICAL CAPACITY CURRENT (FUTURE)
FACILITY & SECTION			
US 15-501			
EPB - SR 1653			(32000)
SR 1653 - SR 1805			(26000)
SR 1805 - NC 24-27			(26000)
NC 24-27 - SR 1802			(26000)
SR 1802 - NC 22			13000
NC 22 - SR 1833			(28000)
SR 1833 - SPB			(28000)
NC 24-27			
US 15-501 - SR 1006			11000
SR 1006 - ECL			(18000)
ECL - SR 1802			(18000)
SR 1802 - NC 22			(18000)
NC 22 - SR 1240			13000
SR 1240 - SR 1644			13000
SR 1644 - WCL			13000
WCL - SR 1261			11000
SR 1261 - WPB			(32000)
NC 22			
US 15-501 - SR 1256			(28000)
SR 1256 - SCL			13000
SCL - Rockingham St.			13000
Rockingham - NC 24-27			13000
NC 24-27 Bypass			
US 15-501 - NC 22			(13000)
NC 22 - SR 1240			(13000)
SR 1240 - SR 1261			(13000)
SR 1261 - NC 22-24-27			(13000)
SR 1006 (Glendon-Carthage Road)			
NPB - SR 1651	1.20	6.7	12000
SR 1651 - NC 24-27	1.94	6.7	12000
NC 24-27 - US 15-501	0.17	6.7	12000
SR 1240 (Dowd Road)			
SPB - SR 1256	1.01	5.5	.9000
SR 1256 - WCL	1.90	6.7	12000
WCL - NC 22-24-27	0.71	12.8	12000

2

Appendix B
reet Tabulation and Recommendations

PRACTICAL CAPACITY CURRENT (FUTURE)	RECOMME X - SEC RDWAY (ULT)
9000	ADQ
9000	ADQ
9000	ADQ
9000	ADQ
9000	ADQ
9000	ADQ
9000	ADQ
11000	ADQ
11000	ADQ
12000	ADQ
12000	ADQ
13000	ADQ
9000	ADQ
9000	ADQ
9000	ADQ
11000	ADQ
12000	ADQ
9000	ADQ

Appendix B
Thoroughfare Plan Street Tabulation and Recomm

FACILITY & SECTION	PRACTICAL CAPACITY CURRENT (FUTURE)
McNeil St.	
NC 24-27 - Summit St.	13000
Saunders Street	
Ray Street - SR 1240	(18000)
SR 1240 - NC 22	(18000)
NC 22 - Rockingham St	(18000)
Rockingham St - SR 1802	(18000)
Rockingham Street	
NC 22 - NC 24-27	11000
Summit Street	
SR 1651 - McNeil St.	11000
Ray Street	
NC 24-27 - Saunders St.	(18000)
Saunders St - Barret St	(18000)
Barret Street	
NC 24-27 - Ray St.	(18000)

4

Appendix C

Typical Cross Sections

r thoroughfares vary according to the desired capacity and level of
rsal standards in the design of thoroughfares are not practical. Each
ally analyzed and its cross section requirements determined on the
ojected traffic, existing capacity, desired level of service, and
al cross section recommendations are shown in Figure C-1. These
acilities on new location and where right-of-way constraints are not
s and urban projects with limited right-of-way, special cross sections
t the needs of the project.

ss sections shown in Appendix B, Table B-1 were derived on the
ting capacities, desirable levels of service, and available right-of-

major thoroughfares delineated on the thoroughfare plan, adequate
ted or acquired for the ultimate cross sections. Ultimate desirable
thoroughfares are listed in Appendix B. Recommendations for
rovided for the following:

require widening after the current planning period
orderline adequate and accelerated traffic growth could render

ban curb and gutter cross section may be locally desirable because
edevelopment.

rds relating to grades, sight distances, degree of curve, super
ations for thoroughfares are given in Appendix D.

h Median - Freeway

highways in rural areas which may have only partial or no control of
n width for this cross section is 14 m (46 feet), but a wider median is

Gutter

mmended for new projects. When the conditions warrant six lanes,
ecommended. Cross section "B" should be used only in special
ning from a five lane section and right-or-way is limited. Even in
n should be given to converting the center turn lane to a median so
mal cross section.

utter

res, this cross section is desirable where frequent left turns are
ting development or frequent street intersections.

1   Appendix C

D - Six Lanes Divided with Raised Median - Curb & Gutter/ E - Four Lanes Divide Raised Median - Curb & Gutter

These cross sections are typically used on major thoroughfares where left turns and inter streets are not as frequent. Left turns would be restricted to a few selected intersections. 4.8 m (16 ft) median is the minimum recommended for an urban boulevard type cross se most instances, monolithic construction should be utilized due to greater cost effectivene and speed of placement, and reduced future maintenance requirements. In special cases, or landscaped medians result in greatly increased maintenance costs and an increase dan maintenance personnel. Non-monolithic medians should only be recommended when th concerns are addressed.

F - Four Lanes Divided - Boulevard, Grass Median

Recommended for urban boulevards or parkways to enhance the urban environment and improve the compatibility of major thoroughfares with residential areas. A minimum m width of 7.3 m (24 ft) is recommended with 9.1 m (30 ft) being desirable.

G - Four Lanes - Curb & Gutter

This cross section is recommended for major thoroughfares where projected travel indic need for four travel lanes but traffic is not excessively high, left turning movements are l right-of-way is restricted. An additional left turn lane would probably be required at ma intersections. This cross section should be used only if the above criteria is met. If righ is not restricted, future strip development could take place and the inner lanes could bec facto left turn lanes.

H - Three Lanes - Curb & Gutter

In urban environments, thoroughfares which are proposed to function as one-way traffic would typically require cross section "H".

I - Two Lanes - C&G, Parking both sides: J - Two Lanes - C&G, Parking one side

Cross sections "I" and "J" are usually recommended for urban minor thoroughfares sinc facilities usually serve both land service and traffic service functions. Cross section "I" used on those minor thoroughfares where parking on both sides is needed as a result of intense development.

K - Two Lanes - Paved Shoulder

This cross section is used in rural areas or for staged construction of a wider multi-lane section. On some thoroughfares, projected traffic volumes may indicate that two travel adequately serve travel for a considerable period of time. For areas that are growing an widening will be necessary, the full right-of-way of 30 m (100 ft) should be required. I instances, local ordinances may not allow the full 30 m. In those cases, 21 m (70 ft) sh preserved with the understanding that the full 30 m will be preserved by use of buildin and future street line ordinances.

L - Six Lanes Divided with Grass Median - Freeway

Cross section "L" is typical for controlled access freeways. The 14 m (46 ft) grassed m minimum desirable median width, but there could be some variation from this dependi design considerations. Right-of-way requirements would typically vary upward from 7 (228 ft) depending upon cut and fill requirements.

2 · Ap

M - Eight Lanes Divided with Raised Median - Curb & Gutter

Also used for controlled access freeways, this cross section may be recommended for freeways going through major urban areas or for routes projected to carry very high volumes of traffic.

N - Five Lanes/C&G, Widened Curb Lanes; O - Two Lane/Shoulder Section; P - Four Lanes Divided/Raised Median, C&G, Widened Curb Lanes

If there is sufficient bicycle travel along the thoroughfare to justify a bicycle lane or bikeway, additional right-of-way may be required to contain the bicycle facilities. The North Carolina Bicycle Facilities Planning and Design Guidelines should be consulted for design standards for bicycle facilities. Cross sections "N", "O", and "P" are typically used to accommodate bicycle travel.

General

The urban curb and gutter cross sections all illustrate the sidewalk adjacent to the curb with a buffer or utility strip between the sidewalk and the minimum right-of-way line. This permits adequate setback for utility poles. If it is desired to move the sidewalk farther away from the street to provide additional separation for pedestrians or for aesthetic reasons, additional right-of-way must be provided to insure adequate setback for utility poles.

The right-of-ways shown for the typical cross sections are the minimum rights-of-way required to contain the street, sidewalks, utilities, and drainage facilities. Cut and fill requirements may require either additional right-of-way or construction easements. Obtaining construction easements is becoming the more common practice for urban thoroughfare construction.

TYPICAL THOROUGHFARE CROSS SECTIONS

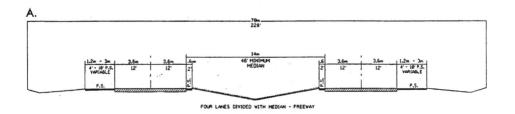

A.

FOUR LANES DIVIDED WITH MEDIAN - FREEWAY

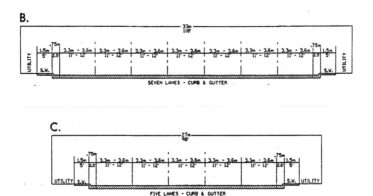

B.

SEVEN LANES - CURB & GUTTER

C.

FIVE LANES - CURB & GUTTER

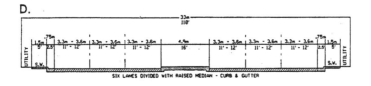

D.

SIX LANES DIVIDED WITH RAISED MEDIAN - CURB & GUTTER

TYPICAL THOROUGHFARE CROSS S

E.

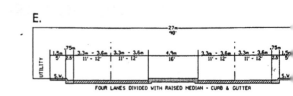

FOUR LANES DIVIDED WITH RAISED MEDIAN - CURB & GUTTER

F.

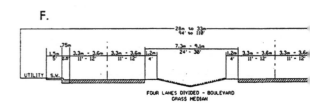

FOUR LANES DIVIDED - BOULEVARD
GRASS MEDIAN

G.   **H.**

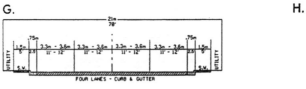

FOUR LANES - CURB & GUTTER

THR

I.   **J.**

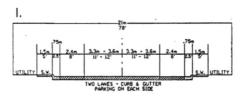

TWO LANES - CURB & GUTTER
PARKING ON EACH SIDE

TWO
P

K.

TWO LANES - PAVED SHOULDER

SIX LANES DIVIDED WITH GRASS MEDIAN - FREEWAY

EIGHT LANES DIVIDED WITH RAISED MEDIAN - CURB & GUTTER

TYPICAL THOROUGHFARE CROSS SECTIONS
FOR ACCOMMODATING BICYCLES

N.

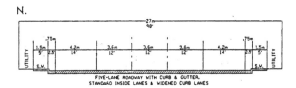

FIVE-LANE ROADWAY WITH CURB & GUTTER,
STANDARD INSIDE LANES & WIDENED CURB LANES

O.

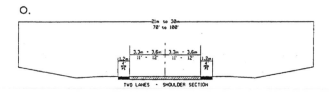

TWO LANES - SHOULDER SECTION

P.

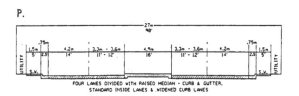

FOUR LANES DIVIDED WITH RAISED MEDIAN - CURB & GUTTER,
STANDARD INSIDE LANES & WIDENED CURB LANES

Appendix D

Recommended Subdivision Ordinances

s

nd Roads

l'Arterial - A rural link in a highway system serving travel, and having characteristics e of substantial statewide or interstate travel and existing solely to serve traffic. This would consist of Interstate routes and other routes designated as principal arterials.

rterial - A rural roadway joining cities and larger towns and providing intra-state and nty service at relatively high overall travel speeds with minimum interference to movement.

ollector - A road which serves major intra-county travel corridors and traffic rs and provides access to the Arterial system.

ollector - A road which provides service to small local communities and traffic rs and provides access to the Major Collector system.

oad - A road which serves primarily to provide access to adjacent land, over relatively stances.

ets

horoughfares - Major thoroughfares consist of Inter-state, other freeway, expressway, vay roads, and major streets that provide for the expeditious movement of high s of traffic within and through urban areas.

horoughfares - Minor thoroughfares perform the function of collecting traffic from cess streets and carrying it to the major thoroughfare system. Minor thoroughfares used to supplement the major thoroughfare system by facilitating minor through novements and may also serve abutting property.

treet - A local street is any street not on a higher order urban system and serves y to provide direct access to abutting land.

pe Rural or Urban Streets

y, expressway, or parkway - Divided multilane roadways designed to carry large s of traffic at high speeds. A *freeway* provides for continuous flow of vehicles with no ccess to abutting property and with access to selected crossroads only by way of nges. An *expressway* is a facility with full or partial control of access and generally de separations at major intersections. A *parkway* is for non-commercial traffic, with artial control of access.

2. *Residential Collector Street* - A local street which serves as a connector street between loc
   residential streets and the thoroughfare system. Residential collector streets typically coll
   traffic from 100 to 400 dwelling units.

3. *Local Residential Street* - Cul-de-sacs, loop streets less than 760 meters (2500 ft) in length
   streets less than 1.6 kilometers (1.0 miles) in length that do not connect thoroughfares, or
   serve major traffic generators, and do not collect traffic from more than 100 dwelling units

4. *Cul-de-sac* - A short street having only one end open to traffic and the other end being
   permanently terminated and a vehicular turn-around provided.

5. *Frontage Road* - A road that is parallel to a partial or full access controlled facility and
   provides access to adjacent land.

6. *Alley* - A strip of land, owned publicly or privately, set aside primarily for vehicular servic
   access to the back side of properties otherwise abutting on a street.

Property

Building Setback Line

A line parallel to the street in front of which no structure shall be erected.

Easement

A grant by the property owner for use by the public, a corporation, or person(s), of a strip of la
for a specific purpose.

Lot

A portion of a subdivision, or any other parcel of land, which is intended as a unit for transfer
ownership or for development or both. The word "lot" includes the words "plat" and "parcel"

Subdivision

Subdivider

Any person, firm, corporation or official agent thereof, who subdivides of develops any land
deemed to be a subdivision.

Subdivision

All divisions of a tract or parcel of land into two or more lots, building sites, or other division
the purpose, immediate or future, of sale or building development and all divisions of land
involving the dedication of a new street or change in existing streets.

The following shall not be included within this definition nor subject to these regulations:

* The combination or re-combination of portions of previously platted lots where the total
  number of lots is not increased and the resultant lots are equal to or exceed the standards
  contained herein
* the division of land into parcels greater than 4 hectares (10 acres) where no street right-of-
  way dedication is involved

cquisition, by purchase, of strips of land for the widening or the opening of streets
of a tract in single ownership whose entire area is no greater than 0.8
acres) into not more than three lots, where no street right-of-way dedication is
d where the resultant lots are equal to or exceed the standards contained herein.

owner, of his property to another party without any consideration being given for
he dedication is made by written instrument and is completed with an acceptance.

f land does not involve any transfer of property rights. It constitutes an obligation
rty free from development for a stated period of time.

STANDARDS

d Roads

all roads within the Planning Area shall be in accordance with the accepted policies
arolina Department of Transportation, Division of Highways, as taken or modified
ican Association of State Highway Officials' (AASHTO) manuals.

of street rights-of-way shall conform and meet the recommendations of the
Plan, as adopted by the municipality. The proposed street layout shall be
ith the existing street system of the surrounding area. Normally the proposed streets
extension of existing streets if possible.

Widths

(ROW) widths shall not be less than the following and shall apply except in those
ROW requirements have been specifically set out in the Thoroughfare Plan.

er will only be required to dedicate a maximum of 30 meters (100 ft) of right-of-way.
e over 30 meters (100 ft) of right-of-way is desired, the subdivider will be required
e the amount in excess of 30 meters (100 ft). On all cases in which right-of-way is
ully controlled access facility, the subdivider will only be required to make a
t is strongly recommended that subdivisions provide access to properties from
s, and that direct property access to major thoroughfares, principle and minor
major collectors be avoided. Direct property access to minor thoroughfares is also

th right-of-way, not less than 18 meters (60 ft) in width, may be dedicated when
leveloped property that is owned or controlled by the subdivider; provided that the
rtial dedication be such as to permit the installation of such facilities as may be
serve abutting lots. When the said adjoining property is sub-divided, the remainder
uired right-of-way shall be dedicated.

Table D-1

	Minimum Right-of-way Requirements	
Area Classification	Functional Classification	Minimum ROW
RURAL	Principle Arterial	Freeways- 105 m (350 Other- 60 m (200 ft)
	Minor Arterial	30 m (100 ft)
	Major Collector	30 m (100 ft)
	Minor Collector	24 m (80 ft)
	Local Road	18 m1 (60 ft)
URBAN	Major Thoroughfare	27 m (90 ft)
	Minor Thoroughfare	21 m (70 ft)
	Local Street	18 m1 (60 ft)
	Cul-de-sac	variable2

[1]The desirable minimum right-of-way (ROW) is 18 meters (60 ft). If curb and gutter i provided, 15 meters (50 ft) of ROW is adequate on local residential streets.

[2]The ROW dimension will depend on radius used for vehicular turn around. Distance of pavement of turn around to ROW should not be less than distance from edge of p ROW on street approaching turn around.

Street Widths

Widths for street and road classifications other than local shall be as recommended by Thoroughfare Plan. Width of local roads and streets shall be as follows:

1. *Local Residential*

> * Curb and Gutter section
>> * 7.8 meters (26 ft), face to face of curb
> * Shoulder section
>> * 6 meters (20 ft) to edge of pavement, 1.2 meters (4 ft) for should

2. *Residential Collector*

> * Curb and Gutter section
>> * 10.2 meters (34 ft), face to face of curb
> * Shoulder section
>> * 6 meters (20 ft) to edge of pavement, 1.8 meters (6 ft) for should

A

ics

low shall apply to all subdivision streets proposed for addition to the
Municipal Street System. In cases where a subdivision is sought
)roughfare corridor, the requirements of dedication and reservation
Way shall apply.

design speed for a roadway should be a minimum of 10 km/h (5 mph)
l speed limit. The design speeds for subdivision type streets are shown in
id D-3 (english).

ance - In the interest of public safety, no less than the minimum sight
all be provided. Vertical curves that connect each change in grade shall
lated using the parameters set forth in Tables D-4 (metric) and D-5

bles D-6 (metric) and D-7 (english) show the minimum radius and the
:relevation for design speeds. The maximum rate of roadway
rural roads with no curb and gutter is 0.08. The maximum rate of
an streets with curb and gutter is 0.06, with 0.04 being desirable.

num Grades

um grades in percent are shown in Table D-8 (metric) and D-9 (english)
grade should not be less then 0.5%
30 meters (100 ft) each way from intersections (measured from edge of
should not exceed 5%

Table D-2

Design Speeds (Metric)

| Desirable | Design Speed (km/h) | | |
| | Minimum | | |
	Level		Rolling
100	80		60
80	80		60
100	60		60
100	50		50
50	50		30

Residential Collectors and Local Residential.

)ther than Freeways or Expressways.

5   **Appendix D**

| Facility Type | Design Speed (mph) | | |
| | Desirable | Minimum | |
		Level	Rolling
RURAL			
Minor Collector Roads	60	50	40
(ADT Over 2000)			
Local Roads1			
(ADT Over 400)	50	* 50	* 40
URBAN			
Major Thoroughfares2	60	50	40
Minor Thoroughfares	40	30	30
Local Streets	30	** 30	** 20

Note: *Based on ADT of 400-750. Where roads serve a limited area and small number of units can reduce minimum design speed. **Based on projected ADT of 50-250. (Reference NCDOT Roadway Design Manual page 1-1B)

1Local Roads including Residential Collectors and Local Residential.

2Major Thoroughfares other than Freeways or Expressways.

Table D-4

30	30	29.6	3	4
50	70	57.4	9	11
60	90	74.3	14	15
90	170	131.2	43	30
100	210	157.0	62	37

Note: General practice calls for vertical curves to be multiples of 10 meters. Calculated length shall be rounded up in each case. *Minimum passing distance for 2-lanes is currently un revision. (Reference NCDOT Roadway Metric Design Manual page 1-12 T-1)

1K is a coefficient by which the algebraic difference in grade may be multiplied to determin length of the vertical curve which will provide the desired sight distance. Sight distance provided for stopped vehicles at intersections should be in accordance with "A Policy on Geometric Design of Highways and Streets, 1990".

ance (English)

Minimum K Values (feet)		Passing Sight Distance (feet)
Crest Curve	Sag Curve	For 2-lanes
30	40	1100
60	60	1500
110	90	1800
190	120	2100

ves to be multiples of 50 feet. Calculated lengths shall
ice NCDOT Roadway Design Manual page 1-12 T-1)

difference in grade may be multiplied to determine the
:ovide the desired sight distance. Sight distance
tions should be in accordance with "A Policy on
ets, 1990".

ble D-6

Minimum Radius of Maximum e	
e=0.06	e=0.08
90	80
160	145
250	230
435	395

r per meter

ble D-7

tion Table (English)

f Maximum e	Maximum Degree of Curve		
e=0.08	e=0.04	e=0.06	e=0.08
260	19 00'	21 00'	22 45'
477	10 00'	11 15'	12 15'
819	6 00'	6 45'	7 30'
1,146	3 45'	4 15'	4 45'

per foot

i Manual page 1-12 T-6 thru T-8)

Table D-8

Maximum Vertical Grade (Metric)

Facility Type and Design Speed (km/h)		Maximum Grade in Percent	
		Flat	Rolling
RURAL			
Minor Collector Roads*			
	30	7	10
	50	7	9
	65	7	8
	80	6	7
	100	5	6
	110	4	5
Local Roads*1			
	30	-	11
	50	7	10
	65	7	9
	80	6	8
	100	5	6
URBAN			
Major Thoroughfares2			
	50	8	9
	65	7	8
	80	6	7
	100	5	6
Minor Thoroughfares*			
	30	9	12
	50	9	11
	65	9	10
	80	7	8
	100	6	7
	110	5	6
Local Streets*			
	30	-	11
	50	7	10
	65	7	9
	80	6	8
	100	5	6

Note: *For streets and roads with projected annual average daily traffic less than grades less than 150 meters (500 ft) long, grades may be 2% steeper than t above table.(Reference NCDOT Roadway Metric Design Manual page 1-1

1Local Roads including Residential Collectors and Local Residential.

2Major Thoroughfares other than Freeways or Expressways.

8

Table D-9

Maximum Grade in Percent

Flat	Rolling	Mountainous
7	10	12
7	9	10
7	8	10
6	7	9
5	6	8
4	5	6
-	11	16
7	10	14
7	9	12
6	8	10
5	6	-
8	9	11
7	8	10
6	7	9
5	6	8
9	12	14
9	11	12
9	10	12
7	8	10
6	7	9
5	6	7
-	11	16
7	10	14
7	9	12
6	8	10
5	6	-

rojected annual average daily traffic less than 250 or short
(500 ft) long, grades may be 2% steeper than the values in the
)OT Roadway Metric Design Manual page 1-12 T-3)

il Collectors and Local Residential.

Freeways or Expressways.

Intersections

1. Streets shall be laid out so as to intersect as nearly as possible at right angles, and n should intersect any other street at an angle less than sixty-five (65) degrees.

2. Property lines at intersections should be set so that the distance from the edge of pa the street turnout, to the property line will be at least as great as the distance from t pavement to the property line along the intersecting streets. This property line can established as a radius or as a sight triangle. Greater offsets from the edge of pavel property lines will be required, if necessary, to provide sight distance for the stopp on the side street.

3. Off-set intersections are to be avoided. Intersections which cannot be aligned shou separated by a minimum length of 60 meters (200 ft) between survey centerlines.

Cul-de-sacs

Cul-de-sacs shall not be more than one hundred and fifty (150) meters (500 ft) in leng distance from the edge of pavement on the vehicular turn around to the right-of-way li not be less than the distance from the edge of pavement to right-of-way line on the str approaching the turn around. Cul-de-sacs should not be used to avoid connection witl existing street or to avoid the extension of an important street.

Alleys

1. Alleys shall be required to serve lots used for commercial and industrial purposes ε this requirement may be waived where other definite and assured provisions are m: service access. Alleys shall not be provided in residential subdivisions unless nec unusual circumstances.

2. The width of an alley shall be at least 6.0 meters (20 ft).

3. Dead-end alleys shall be avoided where possible, but if unavoidable, shall be prov adequate turn around facilities at the dead-end as may be required by the Planning

Permits For Connection To State Roads

An approved permit is required for connection to any existing state system road. Thi required prior to any construction on the street or road. The application is available a of the District Engineer of the Division of Highways.

Offsets To Utility Poles

Poles for overhead utilities should be located clear of roadway shoulders, preferably at least 9.0 meters (30 ft) from the edge of pavement. On streets with curb and gutter shall be set back a minimum distance of 1.8 meters (6 ft) from the face of curb.

Wheel Chair Ramps

All street curbs being constructed or reconstructed for maintenance purposes, traffic repairs, correction of utilities, or altered for any reason, shall provide wheelchair ram physically handicapped at intersections where both curb and gutter and sidewalks are and at other major points of pedestrian flow.

Horizontal Width on Bridge Deck

1. The clear roadway widths for new and reconstructed bridges serving 2 lane, 2 way traffic should be as follows:

* shoulder section approach

    * under 800 ADT design year - minimum 8.4 meters (28 ft) width face to face of parapets, rails, or pavement width plus 3 meters (10 ft), whichever is greater

    * 800 - 2000 ADT design year - minimum 10.2 meters (34 ft) width face to face of parapets, rails, or pavement width plus 3.6 meters (12 ft), whichever is greater

    * over 2000 ADT design year - minimum width of 12 meters (40 ft), desirable width of 13.2 meters (44 ft) width face to face of parapets or rails

* curb and gutter approach
    * under 800 ADT design year - minimum 7.2 meters (24 ft) face to face of curbs

    * over 800 ADT design year - width of approach pavement measured face to face of curbs.

* where curb and gutter sections are used on roadway approaches, curbs on bridges shall match the curbs on approaches in height, in width of face to face of curbs, and in crown drop. The distance from face of curb to face of parapet or rail shall be a minimum of 450 millimeters (1' 6"), or greater if sidewalks are required

2. The clear roadway widths for new and reconstructed bridges having 4 or more lanes serving undivided two-way traffic should be as follows:

* shoulder section approach - Width of approach pavement plus width of usable shoulders on the approach left and right. (shoulder width 2.4 m (8 ft) minimum, 3 m (10 ft) desirable.)

* curb and gutter approach - Width of approach pavement measured face to face of curbs.

Appendix E

Housing and Employment Data

t	2025 Employment	1995 Housing	2025 Housing
	9	41	51
	20	92	112
	10	39	69
	0	12	22
	59	31	41
	73	42	62
	90	7	7
	17	14	26
	164	21	27
	10	74	83
	19	29	39
	5	13	16
	21	51	61
	15	67	73
	108	30	35
	8	14	34
	172	23	53
	2	64	68
	10	48	54
	0	16	18
	14	40	48
	164	48	63
	230	53	55
	277	12	17
	117	46	49
	239	0	1
	68	2	2
	63	13	13
	11	5	5
	56	6	6
	49	26	28
	34	8	8
	12	8	18
	41	5	8

ppen 1.

destrian Policy Guidelines

y

cedure for implementing the Pedestrian Policy adopted by the
gust 1993. The pedestrian Policy addresses TIP projects and makes
en "considering the needs of pedestrians to avoid creating hazards to
e concept of "facilitating pedestrian movements for other reasons."

ʿned as a situation when pedestrian movements are physically
ces pedestrians to use another mode of transportation or walk in an
l with the automobile traffic) to pass a barrier. The concept of "not
to allow municipalities to have the flexibility to add pedestrian
or in the future after the TIP project is complete. Our current
lly do not create barriers for pedestrian movements. One exception
bridge rail is at the back of the curb.

or Pedestrian Facilities

ate the need for pedestrian facilities based on the degree to which the

ımitment
ion

ıdestrian Traffic

Γ Funding

ɩs

ɩe cost to replace an existing sidewalk which is removed to make

project would create a hazard to existing pedestrian movements, the
ɩ not create the hazard. However, if there is not evidence that a TIP
to existing pedestrian movements, the municipality will need to
movements which will be affected within five years by the hazard

Incidental Projects

Due to the technical difficulty of describing justification for pedestrian facilities, the commi
chose a cost sharing approach to provide cost containment for the pedestrian facilities. The
may share the incremental cost of constructing the pedestrian facilities if the "intent of the c
are met. The DOT will pay a matching share of incidental pedestrian facility total construct
costs up to a cap of no more than 2% of total project construction cost. The matching share
sliding scale based on population as follows:

Table F-1

Incidental Projects Cost Participation Break Down

| Municipal Population | Participation | |
	DOT	Local
> 100,000	50%	50%
50,000 to 100,000	60%	40%
10,000 to 50,000	70%	30%
< 10,000	80%	20%

Funding Caps

Under normal circumstances, the cumulative funding for preventing hazards and providing
incidental pedestrian facilities should not exceed 2% of the total project construction cost.

Independent Projects

The DOT will have a separate category of money for all independent pedestrian facility pr
North Carolina. The independent pedestrian facility funds will be administered similar to t
Bicycle Program.

Right-of-Way

In general, municipalities are responsible for providing any right-of-way needed to constru
pedestrian facilities. However, the 2.4 meter (8 foot) berm the DOT generally provides on
curb and gutter facilities can accommodate pedestrian facilities.

Maintenance

Local governments will be responsible for maintaining all pedestrian facilities.

For further information about the Pedestrian Policy Guidelines please contact the followin

Statewide Planning Branch
NC Department of Transportation
P.O. Box 25201
Raleigh, NC 27611
(919) 733-4705

'Appe

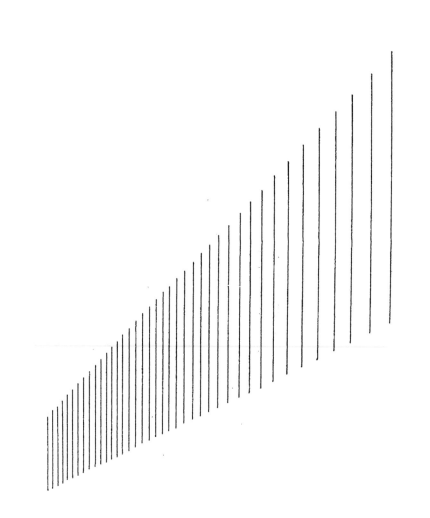

handwritten note at top

STATE OF NORTH CAROLINA
DEPARTMENT OF TRANSPORTATION

AMES B. HUNT JR.
GOVERNOR

DIVISION OF HIGHWAYS
P. O. Box 1067
Aberdeen, North Carolina 28315
August 12, 1996

GARLAND B. GARRETT JR.
SECRETARY

Moore County

Mr. Travis K. Marshall, EIT
Project Engineer
Statewide Planning Branch
P. O. Box 25201
Raleigh, North Carolina 27611-5201

Dear Mr. Marshall:

SUBJECT: Carthage Thoroughfare Plan

Thank you for providing an opportunity for Division review and comment on the Carthage Thoroughfare Plan.

One area of the plan is a source of concern to the Division. That area is the treatment recommended for US 15-501 and its intersection with NC 22. The plan appears to reroute US 15-501 along the proposed NC 24-27 Bypass and an improved section of NC 22. The Division questions whether this recommendation is appropriate. The Division's perspective is the US 15-501 corridor should be maintained on the existing alignment. Improvements to the US 15-501 and NC 22 intersection should be such that NC 22 "T's" into US 15-501. A traffic signal can be considered at this intersection at such time as warrants are satisfied.

Mr. Travis K. Marshall, EIT
August 12, 1996
Page 2

Thank you for your consideration of our comments.

Yours very truly,

F. E. Whitesell, P.E.
DIVISION ENGINEER

cc: Mr. Mary Hayes Holmes
       Mr. J. A. Clendenin
       Mr. W. C. Garner, Jr.

Lightning Source UK Ltd.
Milton Keynes UK
UKHW010945020119
334667UK00006B/83/P